The Singing Accountant's Guide To Tax And Accounts

Everything A Performer Needs To Know
To Keep The Tax Man Happy

Louise Herrington
Performance Accountancy

Printed in the United Kingdom
First Printing September 2018
First Edition

ISBN: 978-1-9996315-6-7 (Print)
ISBN: 978-1-9996315-7-4 (eBook)

Librotas Books
Portsmouth
Hampshire
PO2 9NT

Praise for *The Singing Accountant's Guide To Tax and Accounts*

Where to start? At the beginning I suppose. This book couldn't be laid out any clearer if it tried. From the beginning it sets out its stall. Who would have thought an accountant could explain such a dry and boring subject in such a way? Tips from filling out your very own self-assessment tax return to starting up a business by yourself are in abundance. Starting a business is a daunting task and from a non-accountant's point of view can be seen to be either super easy (that way lies madness) or extremely complicated (thus putting off the quest for world domination).

In this book, the "how to set up your own business" is explained in (not quite) words of one syllable and has the added bonus of knowing there is someone at the end of a phone who can help you through those parts where the words have more than one syllable.

The book is written as if someone is talking to you and explaining things to you as if you were going through the process at the same time. It acknowledges that "doing the books" and tax returns is a bore and a pain but does not dodge from the fact that those things absolutely have to be done. It isn't a book just giving you enough information to be dangerous or not quite enough so that you have to go to the author and pay for their services – as it were. The author genuinely wants you to be able to do these things for yourself.

The book could be a lot longer, which may or may not be a good thing, but I have been assured that another book is in the works which will cover those pesky details such as limited companies, what to do as a director, how to function as a sole trader etc. I am actually looking forward to it!

Michelle Bucknell, Chartered Chemist and Pianist

I have had the pleasure of working with Louise for several years helping her grow and develop her business. Over that time, it has always been clear that she has a real passion for helping her fellow artists and performers understand what they should (and shouldn't) do with regards to their tax issues.

It has been great to see this project evolve from initial idea through to this final book that will be massively useful, not just to the obvious target audience but to the wider small business community in general.

Louise has the ability to take what is a very dry subject and make it entertaining by injecting her own comedy take on things along with a healthy dose of sarcasm. She does this whilst making sure that the advice is clear and well presented.

You will probably recognise yourself in some of the anecdotes and examples throughout the book – if you do, then this book is a must-read for you and your business. Even if you are not an artist or performer, the concepts in this book are very relevant to you and I would suggest that it is an important part of your must-read list for your business.

Chris Waters, Business Mentor (and Grade 1 Piano)

If you are a self-employed creative professional within the arts you should read this book cover to cover. A super accessible and clear account (pun intended) of your obligations to HMRC and how you go about meeting them.

Real insight and information, interspersed with stories and hypotheticals (which offer useful colour and context), all told in Louise's unique voice and inimitable style. Taking a subject like tax returns for creative professionals and making it engaging is not an easy task, and this book manages to be unbelievably thorough whilst managing to avoid being intimidating, or desperately dull.

This should be the starting point for anyone who wants to take the business side of their creative life even vaguely seriously. It offers an overview for the complete novice, but also has insights for those who already have what they might think is a thorough understanding of this subject.

Whatever your level, and however long you've been tackling your tax, this book will help to boost your knowledge of the systems and processes and how they all fit together.

There is so much information out there, from the government, from various accountants and consultants, from friends, from colleges, from colleagues – a lot of it useful, but all from totally separate sources, often with conflicting, outdated, or even wrong information.

When it comes to tax and accounts information, this is one of the first "one stop shops" I've found in my career as an actor and musician.

To have this on the shelf to be able to reference at any given moment when a query comes up regarding the business side of my creative pursuits (and to know the information comes from an experienced, reputable, up–to–date source) is invaluable.

Alex Fobbester – West End Actor

CONTENTS

Section 3: How do I do all this?

Section 4: What else do I need to know?   135

FOREWORD

If there was a female version of Monty Python, this would characterise Louise perfectly. An outrageously blunt, honest and opinionated character who cares, and has a dry sense of humour and talent.

A self-made workaholic who is addicted to ensuring the task in hand is executed with such perfection while ensuring tax is mitigated where possible; and the client understands their situation and circumstances.

This book is aimed at those who "may know a little bit about how register as self-employed", through to those who are more advanced and prepare their accounts on scrap pieces of paper and "shuv" them in an envelope periodically. Then forget to post them or do something for many months. Whether you have a basic, little or no understanding of your accounts and bank statement or you're slightly more advanced, this is something you will be able to dip in and out of, and understand with ease what should be done.

Of course, you don't have to follow her advice – but she will say "told you so".

I write this as a professional myself, who finds accounting dull and boring. With Louise as an advisor and mentor, there really is never a dull moment. From her personal collection of luxury leather goods collected over the years, to her pedantic requirement for printing out every sheet of paper. Ok, she likes to have paperwork to hand and see things printed in black and white. I'm from an era of multiple screens and lots of windows open; she's lemon puffs and sweet white wine; she claims this is a requirement of her singing attributes to ensure the vocal chords are appropriately lubricated – I'm less convinced.

To ignore her would be detrimental to oneself.

Paul Beare, Paul Beare Ltd

INTRODUCTION

Crikey! How do you start an introduction to a book aimed at people in the arts and entertainment industry about tax and accounts as a sole trader? I'd love to be able to tell you that I'm writing this book whilst lying on a beach, feet up, enjoying a cocktail, listening to the sounds of the ocean, but sadly I'm not. I'm sitting here at my desk with *Judge Rinder* on TV in the background. So, let me tell you what this book is about and why you would have picked it up.

This book is for performers who want help to manage their accounts and their tax. I've written it because I generally find that performers, and those with an artistic and creative mind, do not sit happily together with the formal, starchy, rule-ridden state of accounting and tax. Organisation often goes out of the window and there is just no time to keep on top of paperwork.

Most of the time, musicians, singers, dancers, actors and others in this industry only have the option of being self-employed, so you are just thrown in the deep end without much of a life ring to keep you afloat, and I'm sure that you really don't want the tax man beating a path to your door.

This whole thing about being self-employed is confusing, time consuming, and quite frankly a worry. You didn't set out to be an accountant or bookkeeper, so it's probably the last thing you want to do. If it was so important, why wasn't it taught in college and why weren't you told to attend a series of seminars about it? Both of these would have ensured that you would have been better prepared when leaving college.

These are the pain points most people come to me with:

- ♫ How do you set up as self-employed with HMRC?
- ♫ What records do you need to keep?
- ♫ How do you keep the records and for how long?
- ♫ What income needs to be declared?
- ♫ What expenses can I claim for?
- ♫ What is this payment on account HMRC are asking for?

All these questions are covered in the book, and many more besides, with myths and stories from clients over the last few years. By the way, if you're an existing client reading this, and you recognise a problem or story, please don't think it's you. It might well be, but please don't take offence as it could well be about someone else with the same challenge! Don't worry, no names will be mentioned.

I've written this book because over the years, lots of clients have come to me with the above issues, and even the few 90-minute classes I teach at some conservatoires and colleges only cover the basics as there's only so much I can fit into 90 minutes!

As a performer myself, a member of the arts and entertainment industry, as well as a Chartered Accountant, I have seen and experienced first-hand the problems people encounter and how the lack of the correct tax knowledge can hamper people's creativity. I've been in the green room relaxing before my next aria is due, watching people scratching their heads at their piles of paperwork, cursing themselves that they can't remember what an expense was for or why it was incurred. I saw this as an opportunity to help my fellow performers.

So here it is, the answer to all your prayers! I mainly work with singers, musicians, actors and fellow performers in dealing with their accounts and tax, and this is my spiritual home given I still work as a singer (outside tax filing silly season).

This book takes you through a logical progression on what to do when starting out in the world of self-employment, the records you need to keep and suggestions on how to keep them, things that you need to know that may affect your accounts and tax, and finally onto a very brief overview on the tax return itself.

It is an ideal guide for anyone starting out in the business, whether you have just left college or have decided to become a performer as a second career. It is also useful if you've been a performer for a while but struggle to understand accounting and tax. I've written it so that it can be useful for you to dive into sections when you don't understand some of the jargon you hear, for example "payment on account", or "capital allowances". At the end of most chapters, there is a checklist of things you need to know or do – even if you do nothing else.

It is well worth reading (most of) this book cover to cover – it will take about three to four hours but it will give you complete confidence in tackling your accounts and tax, and a total understanding of your obligations, possibly what an accountant may do for you or even your agent, and how they can help you. After you've done that, feel free to pop in and out of chapters. It will make you a more rounded businessperson and a much better freelancer.

As I've mentioned, this book is specifically aimed towards performers – actors, singers, musicians, dancers – and all other people front of house as performers in the arts and entertainment industry. Don't worry if you are one of the wonderful backstage people; there will be a separate book for you.

Now I do give you a word of warning. If you haven't already noticed, I do have a very cynical sense of humour and that may come over in my writing. Well you might find accounting boring – although very necessary – so I'd like to make you smile as you read!

Please note that we cannot assume legal liability for any errors or omissions this information may contain.

SECTION 1:

Do you know if you are really self-employed?

Myth:

I get a payslip each week, so I must be employed.

Fact:

Not necessarily. Some opera companies, film companies, orchestras and schools will "employ" proper employees and self-employed people and pay everybody through the payroll system as a payment method. Gee, this can be confusing. It's often a case of looking at your payslip to see if any tax and National Insurance has been deducted, but if you don't earn enough in the week/month to have any deducted, you still can be confused as to your employment status. The giveaway is if the tax code shows as "NT" (no tax) and National Insurance number as "X"; then you know that payroll is running you as a self-employed person.

CHAPTER 1:

What is the difference between being employed and self-employed?

Be warned – this subject is VERY dry. To establish whether you are employed or self-employed, it is not just a case of whether you work for more than one client or employer. It is all about the working relationship with the business and your contractual position with them. This relationship is looked at seriously by HMRC as they would prefer everybody to be employed so that they can collect tax monthly through the pay as you earn (PAYE) scheme.

The tax man has drawn up a set of business entity tests available online, which are marked by a scoring system. The system just gives a risk factor (high, medium or low) as to whether there could be an investigation. BUT this is not tax law and merely the tax man's view of the risk of falling foul of certain tax rules.

So, the difference between employees and the self-employed is as follows:

Employees	Self-Employed
You have a contract of employment with an employer and the employer dictates what work is to be done, where it is done, when it is performed, and provides the tools to do so.	You have a form of services contract with another person or company, but the self-employed person has influence over the where, when and how the task or service is carried out, or even if they do it and whether they can get somebody else to do the task.
You are taxed on earnings at source from employment during the current tax year.	You are taxed on earnings based on the year end date which is trading income. It is assessed after business costs have been taken into account. If the individual year ends on 30 October 2019, then those earnings are assessed to be for the year 2019/20, which will have to be paid by 31 January 2021.
You are given a P60 or P45 which will show what payments have been made and tax deducted. If expenses are paid or benefits received, you will also get a P11D or P9D.	You write up your own set of accounts which are used to complete the self-assessment tax return.
Your employer is responsible for deducting tax and Class 1 National Insurance prior to wages/salary paid. You get Class 1 National Insurance (NI) which gives entitlement to benefits.	You are responsible for all income tax payments as well as Class 2 and Class 4 NI. Class 2 NI gives you entitlement to state pension but no other benefits. Class 4 NI does nothing for you!
You may have to complete a self-assessment tax return if a higher rate taxpayer of if there is other untaxed income in the year.	You will have to complete a self-assessment tax return.

Employees	Self-Employed
You can only claim expenses against income that is wholly, exclusively and necessarily incurred in the duties of employment.	You can claim expenses against income that is wholly and exclusively incurred in carrying out the business.
The employer takes out insurance for the business.	You may need to take out your own public liability insurance.

The advantages of being self-employed

You might be wondering about the advantages and disadvantages of being self-employed. In my view, here are the advantages:

♪ You have much more flexibility and control over your work, so you can work round other commitments when needed, although sometimes, as performers, we have to take what is offered.

♪ Work can be varied, and you can often be working on several projects at the same time e.g. teaching as well as performing.

♪ Certain costs can be offset against your fee income which helps reduce your tax liability, for example, travel to a temporary workplace as a self-employed person may be offset, whereas employed people cannot claim this. Of course, there are rules that need to be applied for regular places of work that may not be so clear-cut.

♪ Your home can be used as your workplace, and you may be able to offset some home costs against income.

♪ There is a potential to charge higher fees as, being self-employed, as there is no guarantee of work and payment.

The disadvantages of being self-employed

Of course, there are disadvantages of being self-employed, and the biggest one is the risk of not getting any work or not getting paid:

- ♫ Income is not guaranteed, and nor is payment. You may find that you do some work, but it can take weeks or months to receive payment for this work.

- ♫ Finding work can be an issue as can breaking into the area you want to be in.

- ♫ What happens if you get ill or want to take holidays? Of course, that means periods of time without any money coming in that you need to take into account.

- ♫ You need to be highly organised and have the ability to split your work and your personal life, and be able to run your business with administration, bookkeeping, marketing and complying with regulations you may not know about.

- ♫ You should have a separate bank account for your self-employed business as it is easier to know where you are financially, but if you only have self-employed income, then you will need to transfer money between bank accounts.

- ♫ You may end up in the position of all work, no play and find it hard to get a good work–life balance.

Just to note, you may hear the term IR35. IR35 is tax legislation that is designed to combat tax avoidance by workers supplying their services to clients via an intermediary, such as a limited company, but who would be an employee if the intermediary was not used. Such workers are called "disguised employees" by Her Majesty's Revenue and Customs (HMRC). At the moment this only affects people working through their own company, but it is worth keeping an eye on this as HMRC is very interested in these kind of workers, and workers are interested in it as they could be claiming employment benefits such as pension.

The details of IR35 are not dealt with in this book – thank goodness. But you do need to be aware that if you do work through your own limited company and give service to a public company like the BBC, then the off-payrolling rules that came into force in 2017 will affect you, and you will be treated as an employee with tax and National Insurance deducted from your payment. It therefore means there is no point in working through your company for public bodies.

Of course, for most musicians, singers, actors, dancers and other performers, self-employment is the only option, so you need to make sure you set up correctly and as soon as you start to either earn money or spend on your self-employment business. So, read on, McDuff.

Myth:

I don't need to declare any PAYE income on my tax return as it has already been taxed.

Fact:

All income sources need to be on your tax return, unless they are specifically excluded for example ISA interest and some state benefits. Each individual gets one personal allowance and that covers all income sources from employed jobs, self-employment, property income and many other sources.

Things you need to do

☐   Look at your payslips to check for PAYE and NI markers.

☐   Check your contract to see if it says employed or self-employed.

☐   Are you being paid on invoices without deduction?

SECTION 2:

Getting started in this big bad world

Myth:
I've just left music college and I am sure they said I didn't have to do a tax return for two years after leaving.

Reply:
Sadly not – as soon as you are "ready to trade", i.e. earn money from your music or start to spend on getting work that is not employed, then you are classed as self-employed. You need to register with HMRC and start to do a tax return.

It is a story I hear often, and it can lead to fines and penalties of non-filing once you do register with HMRC.

CHAPTER 2:
What is the UK tax system?

For individuals, partnerships and the self-employed, the UK tax year starts on 6 April and finishes on 5 April the following year. I'm normally asked, "Why is that the case? Why can't the UK have 1 April or 1 January?"

This goes back to historical times several hundred years ago, when the tax year end was 25 March, which is why you get quarter days, being 25 March, 24 June, 29 September and 25 December, and that's when a lot of landlords used to get paid and things like that. They are the very old quarter days. This was based on the Julian calendar, and then some time in the 1700s Europe went onto a Gregorian calendar and that meant 11 days were added onto the calendar year.

When the UK changed to the Gregorian calendar, that then pushed the year end to be 5 April, and so that's how we ended up with it. Why it was 25 March I don't know except I think it had religious standing with Lady Day, being 25 March, and Christmas Day being 25 December. Of course, that may be rubbish. Why they haven't decided to follow other countries and have 1 January, I don't know. Anyway, the tax year runs from 6 April to 5 April in the following year.

Basic UK taxes include income tax, property tax, capital gains tax, UK inheritance tax, and also value added tax, which we know as VAT. For the purposes of this book, we're actually only going to be looking at income tax for individuals. The UK tax system applies throughout the UK, so England, Scotland – although at the moment there are some specific differences owing to Scotland's unique legal system – Wales, Northern Ireland, and many of the smaller islands around the British coast. It also includes oil drilling platforms in British territorial waters although it does not include the Channel Islands, the Isle of Man and Republic of Ireland. On the whole, the income tax system treats spouses as separate legal entities and taxes them as individuals, although there is the exception of a small allowance called the marriage allowance that came into place a couple of years ago for income taxes and a couple's marriage allowance for those born before 1935.

Before you can pay taxes in the UK, you need to have a National Insurance number. If you are a British national, this is actually allocated to us on birth and comes into play after we reach our 16th birthday. If you've come from the European Economic Area, or anywhere else actually, you'll have to apply potentially for a tier two visa, and then a National Insurance number will be given to you. If you are not a UK national, the tax status you have is dependent on your residency status, and that'll determine if you actually have to pay UK income tax. I have no intention of going through any of the residency rules. This is something that's completely outside the scope of this book.

What is taxed for UK income tax purposes? Well, I'm going to assume you are resident in the UK for tax purposes, which means that you are taxed on your worldwide income, including foreign investments and savings interest, rental income on overseas properties, and even income from foreign pensions. You then include your everyday items like self-employment, so you'll be taxed on your profit from self-employment. Plus if you have a job that deducts tax at source, commonly known as a PAYE job, that is obviously taxable income. You also need to take into account interest from banks and dividends, and if you've had a PPI claim, the interest from that is taxable. Rental income is taxable, even renting a room to a lodger, as well as property rental and short-term furnished holiday lets. There's not a lot of income that escapes from being taxed. Even if you have a stipend from a church, that would come into taxable income.

The basic premise to working out your tax is you add up all your taxable income, which will be your gross pay from PAYE, your net profit from any self-employment, your net profit from property rental, and any interest paid to you in dividends. Then add it all up together to get to a total income figure. Then subtract your personal allowance, which changes each year, and that results in taxable income. The balance is then multiplied by a certain percentage, determined by how much you earn, and that gives the amount of tax you need to pay.

At the moment, for England, Wales and Northern Ireland, the income tax rates are 20%, 40%, and 45%, and Scotland have done their own thing for rates and levels. For the most up-to-date tax rates and all the bands and income bands, go to our website https://performanceaccountancy.co.uk/rates/ or you can do an internet search for HMRC tax rates and allowances. But it does not end there. For the self-employed, you may have to pay National Insurance on your profits, and for those people with a high enough tax bill, you may have to make a payment on account. I'll tell you more about this in Chapter 27.

As I've already stated, everybody who earns money in the UK as a UK resident must pay tax, but it's dependent on the level. After all, your personal allowance may cover all taxable income, and then income tax is not payable (ignoring National Insurance for the moment). Tax is paid even if you are a child, a pensioner, or just the average Joe down the street. This, of course, can be confusing to some students, as I often have them say to me, "But we don't pay tax". What students are not paying is council tax whilst they are in full-time education. Oh boy, you will be paying tax. If you earn enough.

Now, if you are an employee in the UK, the employer will take regular deductions from your income, and they will pay over your income tax liability and National Insurance direct to HMRC. However, if you have worldwide income, some other income coming in, or you are self-employed – which I imagine is the case, because that's why you're reading this book – then you will have to complete a self-assessment tax return. This looks at not only your PAYE income, but also all of your other sources of income, and then it will determine which tax bracket you are in.

What can happen is you pay tax on a PAYE job, but you might make a loss in self-employment and theoretically you might be able to get a tax refund, which is always great. You may also get a tax refund if you stopped employed work partway through the year. The tax man will do something called a P800 tax calculation, and that happens somewhere between June and October. You might be lucky enough to get a rebate. Woo hoo!

National Insurance for the self-employed

When you first start out in business as a self-employed person, you must tell the HMRC that you have set up in business and register to pay Class 2 National Insurance. This can be done by phone or on part of the online forms for registering as self-employed – this is covered in the section on setting up as self-employed.

As a self-employed person, you must pay Class 2 National Insurance if you are over the minimum income, and then pay Class 4 National Insurance if your profits are over a certain level.

There are various types of National Insurance:

Class 1 is when you are employed, and your employer deducts the amount from your salary prior to you getting paid.

Class 2 has a weekly rate which has to be paid irrespective of whether you have worked that week or have any income. This counts towards your basic state pension and some benefits (sick pay, maternity allowance and bereavement benefit) and it is collected at the same time you pay your self-assessment tax return. You do not have to pay this if you have small profits, but I always advise people that they should consider paying it if they remain in this country and would like to draw a pension of some sort when they reach state pension age. Other exemptions exist if you are under 16 years old, at or over state pension age, or are not resident in the UK.

Class 2 contributions do not normally count towards the additional state pension, statutory sick pay, jobseeker's allowance or employment support allowance, so you might want to think about making other arrangements like a personal pension and income protection insurance.

However, Class 2 NI is earmarked to go from April 2019, and at the time of writing we are not sure what part of Class 4 NI will go towards benefits and pension.

Class 3 NI is for people who want to make additional contributions in the year. These are taken monthly or quarterly and for a set amount per week. It is usually done by people needing to plug holes in the number of contribution years they have as you need to have a minimum of 35 years. These holes can occur if you decide to return to university as a mature student. You can plug the hole providing it is not more than six years ago.

Class 4 NI comes into effect based on profits of your sole trader business. You pay 9% on annual profits between a lower and a higher limit and 2% on any profit over that higher amount. Class 4 NI is calculated when you do your self-assessment tax return and is paid at the same time that your personal tax is paid. It should be noted that Class 4 NI does not contribute towards benefit entitlement. Exceptions to Class 4 NI are noted below. They are the same as Class 2 but with a slightly higher profit level:

- ♫ You are under 16 but you must apply for the exemption on form CA2835U.

- ♫ You are still working in the tax year after you reached state pension age.

- ♫ You are not resident in the UK for tax purposes.

For current rates, please see our website page
https://performanceaccountancy.co.uk/rates/

CHAPTER 3:

What is a self-assessment tax return?

Self-assessment is a system that HM Revenue and Customs, commonly known as HMRC, uses to collect tax. Tax is usually deducted automatically from wages, pensions and savings, but people in business and having other income must report it in their tax return.

There are deadlines in the tax return and, if you're filing online, the deadline is 31 January, following the end of the tax year. Or, if you want to file it by paper, then the deadline is 31 October following the end of the tax year.

You will need to keep fairly detailed records of what income and expenditures you have if you're a self-employed person, and also keep details of what other income you might have received and whether it was taxed at source. If you use the online portal that HMRC provides, it will automatically calculate what you owe.

So, who must send in a tax return? Well, here's a list.

♫ If you were self-employed and your income was more than £1,000 (less than £1,000 is covered by the small trading allowance).

♫ You received more than £2,500 from renting a property (excluding the rent a room scheme limit), but if your income was more than £1,000 and less than £2,500, the helpline can sort you out rather than you having to do a tax return.

♪ You received more than £2,500 of untaxed income. If less than £2,500, you can contact the HMRC helpline and they'll deal with it there.

♪ If your income from savings or investments was £10,000 or more before tax.

♪ If your income from shares was more than £10,000 or more before tax.

♪ If you made profits from selling things like stocks and shares, a second home, any antiques, etc and you potentially might have to pay capital gains tax. It's also a case of if you rented a property and you sold the property, then again, you might have to pay capital gains tax.

♪ If you were a company director, unless it was a not for profit organisation such as a charity and you don't get paid any benefits like a company car. Although this is not in law, so as a director, you don't actually have to do a return if you only have PAYE income. But watch this space!

♪ If your income was over £50,000 and either you or your partner claimed the child benefit.

♪ You also need to do a tax return if you had income from abroad or if you live abroad and have UK income.

♪ Finally, if your taxable income in general was over £100,000, as the personal allowance starts to be taken away from you.

Now, state pension also pops in here. If your state pension was more than the personal allowance and you have no other sources of income for HMRC to take the tax from, then you will need to do a tax return because you have to pay tax on your state pension. This sounds really unfair, doesn't it?!

Myth:

Actors don't pay tax.

Fact:

Everybody should pay tax if their income or profits are greater than the personal allowance. However, you only have to earn over the NI threshold for self-employment, and then there will be a tax bill. The only time actors do not pay tax is if they don't earn enough.

Normally, HMRC will tell you if you need to do a tax return but, potentially, you should have registered first in order for them to tell you to do one. Registering for self-assessment is covered in Chapter 4. But you can go back to HMRC and say you don't think you need to do a tax return, for whatever reason, and you can either do that online or you can do it by phone or post. But if you don't tell HMRC and just ignore it, then they will send you reminders, fines, etc, to file your tax return and, unfortunately, not needing to do one is not a valid excuse if you did not tell them.

There are a few other reasons that you might need to fill in a tax return and that is to claim any tax relief:

- ♪ If you've given money to charity you can obtain relief especially if you're verging on the 20% to 40% tax bracket.

- ♪ If you've made private pension contributions as a higher or additional rate taxpayer or if the pension wasn't set up for automatic relief.

- ♪ If you have work expenses over £2,500.

So, once you have registered for your tax return you should hopefully have access to what we call the Government Gateway, that allows you to go in and do your own tax return via the HMRC software or, of course, you can employ an accountant. Now there are all sorts of reasons why you have to use a paper form, and normally it's if you are doing a tax return for a partnership, for a trust and estate, if you receive income from an estate, if you're a Lloyd's underwriter or if you are a Minister of Religion. But, because this is a book for performers, unless you have one of these other types of income, you can do an online return without any issues.

There are certain deadlines you have to adhere to. If you have not set up as self-employed or to have a self-assessment tax return, then you have until 5 October in the year following when you set up as being self-employed.

So, let's say you set up as being self-employed on 26 June 2019. You have until 5 October 2020 to tell HMRC that you have set up as self-employed and you will need to do a self-assessment tax return. There are deadlines, as already mentioned, for actually filing your return. Please note that HMRC don't need to see any paperwork unless there is an enquiry into your return. Paper tax returns must be received by HMRC by midnight on 31 October 2020 and the online tax returns must be received by midnight, 31 January. Any tax you owe also has to be paid by 31 January. There is an additional payment deadline on 31 July, if you have to make a payment in advance. That's known as payment on account and is dealt with in a separate chapter (Chapter 27).

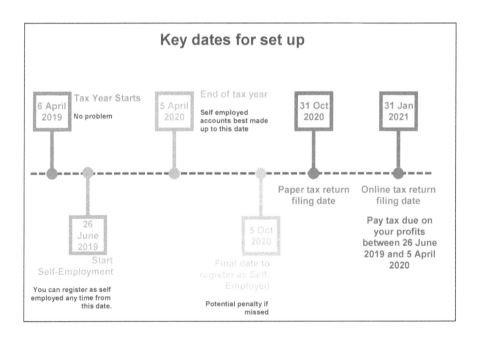

Key dates for set up

6 April 2019 Tax Year Starts — No problem	
5 April 2020 End of tax year — Self employed accounts best made up to this date	
31 Oct 2020	
31 Jan 2021	

26 June 2019 Start Self-Employment — You can register as self employed any time from this date.

5 Oct 2020 Final date to register as Self-Employed — Potential penalty if missed

Paper tax return filing date

Online tax return filing date — Pay tax due on your profits between 26 June 2019 and 5 April 2020

There are cases when you register late with HMRC. Potentially there is a fine or a penalty for registering late, but if you register and there's not three months left until the filing deadline, HMRC normally extend the deadline as to when you have to do your tax return. That is always a bonus, but be aware, they may impose a fine for late registration.

Whilst I'm talking about fines and penalties, if you are late in sending your tax return, either by paper or online, then you get a penalty of £100 and that penalty applies for being up to three months late. If it's more than three months, then the fine goes up, and it starts coming in at £10 a day from 1 May until the next 90 day milestone. Then it goes up by £300 or 5% of the tax due, then another £300 of the tax due after 12 months. You can rack up a lot of fines. So, if you don't realise that you are supposed to have done a tax return, then that's where you get into £1,500 penalties.

Even if you have filed your tax return, especially if you've done it online, you do have the ability to go in and make changes. It might be the case that you filed your tax return on 12 June, knowing that you've actually got until January to file it, but then you've discovered you've missed out some income or some costs. You can still go in and amend the tax return; just remember to re-submit it. There is also a possibility of going in and amending a prior year. You can do that online up to a year beforehand. Again, all this can happen through your HMRC online account.

Any changes prior to that, then it would be a case of writing to HMRC for overpayment relief, and you need to explain to them the tax year you're correcting, why you think you've paid too much or too little tax, how much you think you've over or under paid. And then the reasons for why you're making the change. For example, you might have expected to be paid some dividends, but they didn't actually materialise. So, although you've declared in the tax return that you should have been getting them, you never received them, so therefore you might have been taxed on those dividends but never actually received the money.

Obviously, you can do all this yourself by setting up your own Government Gateway account for self-assessment and registering for self-employed... More on that in the next chapter.

Things you need to do

- ☐ Check if you should be registered for self-assessment. If unsure, call the HMRC and ask them.

CHAPTER 4:

How to register as self-employed

Congratulations, you have made the decision to start up in business on your own. It is a big scary step and you are responsible for EVERYTHING. The good news: you are the boss. The bad news: you are the boss.

You can become self-employed at any stage of your life – whilst at college gigging for concert promoters, in the pit for local societies, when leaving full-time education or employment to make your own way in the world, or even having done a "normal" job and taking the plunge to work at the same time or to leave that stable job behind. Most performers start off as self-employed, unless you are lucky enough to land a job in one of the repertory companies or orchestras. In the first chapter, I discussed the differences between self-employed versus employed, so head back there if you need a refresh.

This section simply lays out what you need to do to register with HMRC so that you comply with the law. Beware though, as the screens often change, and as more and more HMRC services go online, there will be further changes in how to do it and different URLs for the webpages. I first wrote this chapter in 2016, and the pages used then have disappeared, but this is up to date as of June 2018.

Even if you already complete a self-assessment tax return, you still have to tell HMRC you have started a self-employed business. The reason for this is that it sets up your National Insurance record for receiving self-employed contributions. If it is not done in a timely manner, then you are open to penalties. An individual should register as self-employed no later than six months from the end of the tax year they became self-employed. Failure to tell HMRC within the time limit may incur a £100 penalty plus interest. You will see the date is 5 October following the end of the tax year you started to be self-employed.

I briefly mentioned the Government Gateway in the last chapter. You can register online for the Government Gateway, which is often referred to as the digital personal tax account (but there is much more in here than just the ability to do a tax return). I am going to assume you don't already have a Gateway account and you are fresh into the swing of things.

Here we go. Start by going to this website http://bit.ly/NEWSA2017 and that will take you directly to the set-up page that looks like this.

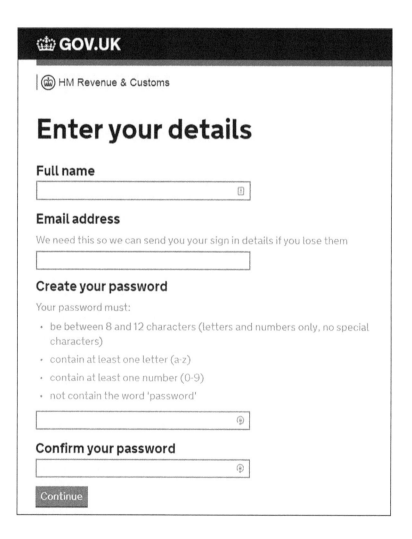

As soon as you do this, the system will generate you a user ID number which you must take note of as this is your access to the system. Oh, the joy you will have if you forget this later in the year – please don't do it!

Then you'll be met with this screen:

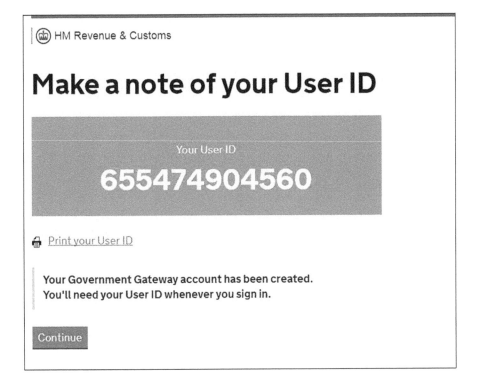

Don't worry – this is just a dummy I have set up and I am not giving away any personal secrets or client data.

If you don't have a permanent physical tax file, this may be the time you start one, and the first bit of paper in there will be this number. Of course, if you are technically sweet, then you could print it to a PDF and store it somewhere safe on your computer.

Having set up the account, you then need to register for HMRC taxes. This may start to look a little daunting but bear with me. Feel free to read all the blurb on this screen, but you are only concerned with telling HMRC that you need to register for a new tax. So, click on that option and hit "Next".

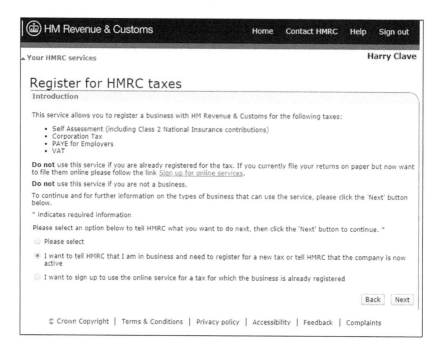

And then they bring up another long screen of stuff, to which you just want to press "Next".

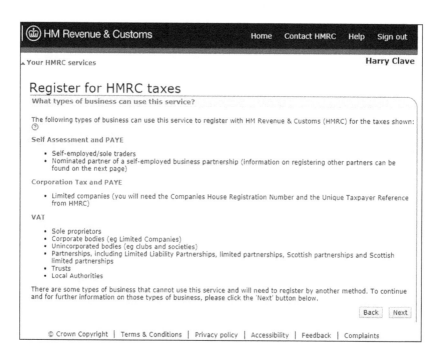

I have no idea where I came up with the test subject name of Harry Clave, but I did. This next screen tells you what you cannot register for via the online service but given I have sent you to this for self-assessment, you are OK to press "Next".

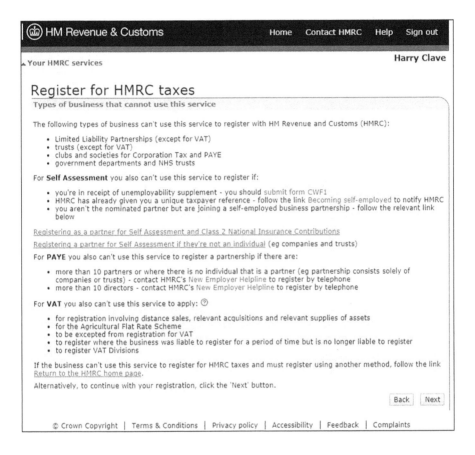

The system then states the obvious that you can only set up taxes if you have a Government Gateway account, but as you already set this up five minutes ago, assuming you have not left your computer, made a cup of tea, and watched *EastEnders*, then you are still likely to be in the Gateway system and have not been thrown out.

Just click "Next" again at this screen.

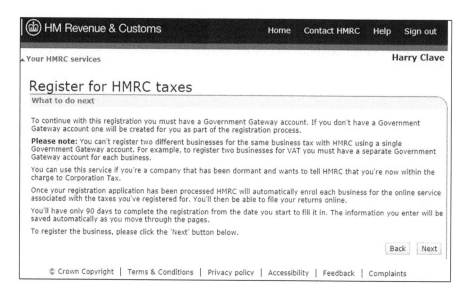

Finally, you'll get to the screen that you wanted in the first place, and that is to set up for self-assessment in order to tell HMRC we are self-employed. Woo hoo.

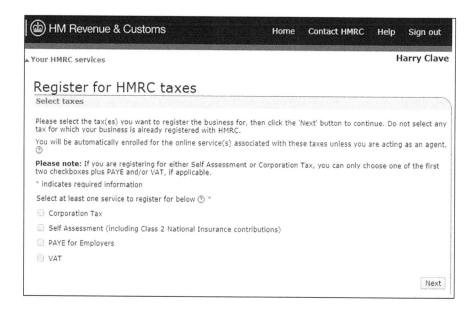

Tick the box that says "Self Assessment" and press "Next".

Oh my – we are getting somewhere.

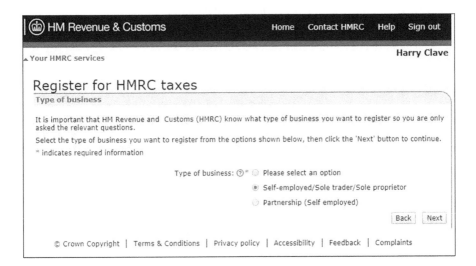

Now we get to tell the system that we are planning on being self-employed. Are you getting excited yet? Select "Self-employed" and press "Next".

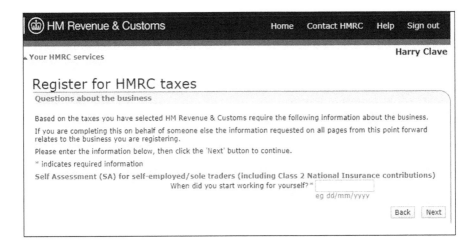

Now I get to the first word of warning: the date you started to work for yourself. I have already said you need to register by 5 October in the tax year following the date you set up, but if you decided you set up on 1 April, then that is in the prior tax year, and you will be expected to do a tax return for that year, even if you haven't traded. If you are setting up in April, please don't set the date between 1 and 5 April, unless you really did incur valid business costs, or invoice people or receive fees in that period.

Next, complete the date you set up and press "Next".

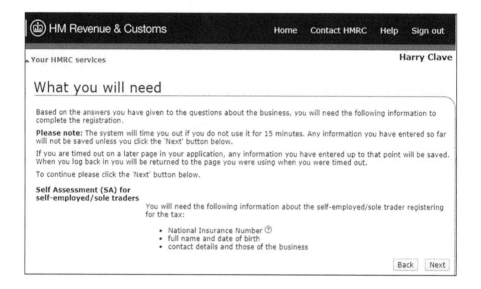

Hopefully you will know your name, date of birth and contact details, but you need to know your National Insurance number before you can proceed. It is a shame the system does not remember your name and email address from the first page, but hey ho.

Click on "Next" and we'll move to the next screen.

Now start to enter the basic information about you. Most of the information will be "No" after the UK resident question, so don't panic.

About you

Business registration

▸ Registration summary

▾ About you
  ▸ Personal information
  ▸ Your home address
  ▸ Your contact details
▸ About the business
▸ View and print
▸ FAQs

Personal information

Please enter the details below about the person who is registering for the tax(es), then click the 'Next' button to continue.

* indicates required information

Title: *

First name: *

Middle name(s):

Last name: *

Have you ever changed your name? * [Please select ▾]

Date of birth: *
eg dd/mm/yyyy

National Insurance Number: *
eg QQ123456A

Are you a UK resident? * [Please select ▾]

If yes, have you come to the UK from a non-EU country within the last 12 months? [Please select ▾]

Are you a share fisherman? * [Please select ▾]

Are you a land and property business? * [Please select ▾]

Are you a Lloyds Underwriter? * [Please select ▾]

Are you a director? * [Please select ▾]

Are you a Minister of Religion - not in receipt of a salary or stipend? * [Please select ▾]

Are you an examiner, invigilator, set examination/test questions under a 'Contract of Service'? * [Please select ▾]

Is your business in Investment? * [Please select ▾]

Do you intend to work in the construction industry? * [Please select ▾]

If you have previously registered for Self Assessment, please enter the Unique Taxpayer Reference you were given at the time. It is the ten digit reference in the top left-hand corner on page one of the tax return.

Previously registered Unique Taxpayer Reference (UTR):
eg 1234567890

If you are working for one person or firm only, you may be employed rather than self-employed. If you are unsure, you can check your employment status using the Employment Status Indicator tool by following the link below.

Employment Status Indicator ▸

Are you working for one person or firm only? * [Please select ▾]

As this is a dummy client, all data entered has been removed but hopefully you will be able to see what the screen will look like once your data has been entered and is shown for checking.

Onwards now to the address screens.

Enter your postcode and then click on "Find address".

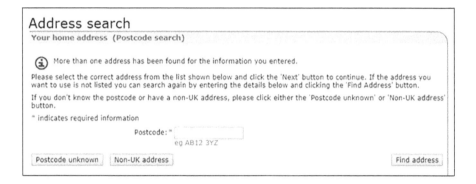

A complete list of all addresses will be shown at that postcode, so you can then select your own address.

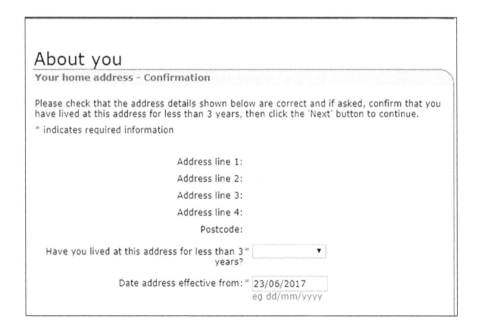

The system will ask the standard identity question regarding if you have moved within three years, so if you have not lived there for more than three years, select "Yes". As musicians and actors, at the start of your career, it is likely that you move to where the work is. Of course, you can use your parental home as the address you are registered at.

If you did answer "Yes" to the address question, another address box pops up to enter your previous address, but it does not ask if that was for less than three years.

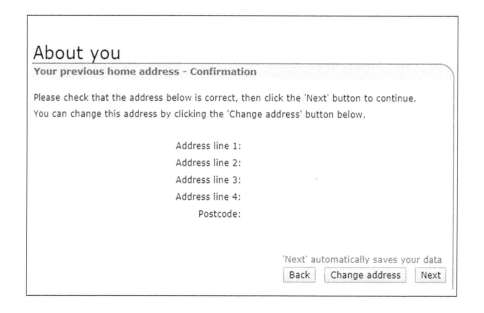

The standing data continues. It then asks for your email address. You've already given your email address once on a few screens ago but it asks for it again and it wants you to confirm your email address to make sure it's correct. You do not have to put in your telephone number or your mobile number, but the next screen asks for this. It is very, very rare for HMRC to phone you. Normally most of the correspondence is done by letter and by post. But at least it's there if they are desperate to get hold of you.

And now we go to see the review of your personal data. This summarises everything you have just entered. Again, as said before, I've deleted everything that was related to my client, but you get to check the data before moving on.

About you

Confirmation

Please check that the information below is correct, then click the 'Next' button to continue. If any of the information is incorrect, follow the link in the section you want to change.

Personal information

Name:	
Date of birth:	
National Insurance Number:	
Are you a UK resident?	Yes
Have you come to the UK from a non-EU country within the last 12 months?	No
Are you a share fisherman?	No
Are you a land and property business?	No
Are you a Lloyds Underwriter?	No
Are you a director?	No
Are you a Minister of Religion - not in receipt of a salary or stipend?	No
Are you an examiner, invigilator, set examination/test questions under a 'Contract of Service'?	No
Is your business in Investment?	No
Do you intend to work in the construction industry?	No
Previously registered Unique Taxpayer Reference (UTR):	Not provided
Are you working for one person or firm only?	No

Change personal information ▶

Home address(es)

Address line 1:	
Address line 2:	
Address line 3:	
Address line 4:	
Postcode:	
Date address effective from:	
Previous address line 1:	
Previous address line 2:	
Previous address line 3:	

So that was all your personal data and now it moves on to what your business data is all about. It's got here again the question, "When did you start working for yourself?" We've already answered that question a few screens ago, so make sure this is the same date. It has the same health warning with what dates you put in, etc.

About the business
Business details

Please answer the questions below relating to the business, then click the 'Next' button to continue.

* indicates required information

When did you start working for yourself? *

eg dd/mm/yyyy

Trading name of the business (if applicable):

What sort of self-employed work do you do? *
(eg plumbers, investment business, electrical engineers):

Your trading name: this is where you might have your birth name and then an Equity name. You can put in your birth name, say Joe Cataract (I don't know why I thought of that), but you may actually trade under Joe Eye so that would be what you put in the "Trading name" box. What sort of self-employed work do you do? Now a lot of people just put down "Actor". It does then limit your scope because you might decide that you're an actor and a drama teacher, so I'd put both in. You are a musician and a music teacher. You are an actor and a voiceover artist. So if you do mix it up into a bit of a portfolio of income for self-employment, then just put what you need in there. That way if you then start to claim expenses for one of these other jobs you haven't listed and HMRC look at your tax return, you can state that you declared you were a voiceover artist. That's why you've been purchasing mics and cladding. Click "Next" to continue.

About the business

Business address

You entered the address shown below as the home address of the person registering for the tax(es). Please confirm if the business address is the same by selecting an option from the drop-down menu.

* indicates required information

Address line 1:

Address line 2:

Address line 3:

Address line 4:

Postcode:

Is the business address the same as this* address?   Please select ▼

Again, it asks for the address. So what is your business address? For most of us in our profession, our business address is our home address. But still check it out with any landlords, etc, if you rent your property, as to whether you can run your business from home. But most of the time it's our home address and you have to enter it again. Is the business address the same as this address? Well yes, the answer's going to be "Yes".

About the business

Business contact details

Please enter details that HM Revenue & Customs (HMRC) can use to contact you about the business.

If you enter an email address confirmation of receipt of your registration can be sent to you.

* indicates required information

Please provide at least one of the following contact details: *

Business telephone number (including STD):

Business mobile telephone number:

Business fax number (including STD):

Please note: You must provide an email address if you want HMRC to send you an email acknowledging receipt of your registration.

Business email address:

Confirm business email address:

And again, you've got the option of entering your data for the email address and telephone number, but it does need to have at least one of the telephone numbers completed. All right, so click "Next" to continue.

The system then displays your business data so you can check to ensure everything's correct. There are options of going back to various different screens if something is not correct. Now when you've completed this bit, this is for the self-employment side. The bit at the bottom says that it will automatically register you for self-assessment online. That gives you the ability to do your self-assessment tax return directly on the Government Gateway. So never tick the box to say that you want to be removed from it. You don't want to say no, because you want to have access to the self-assessment online. So do not tick that box. I know we're all tempted to tick boxes but do not tick that box. What don't you do? Correct.

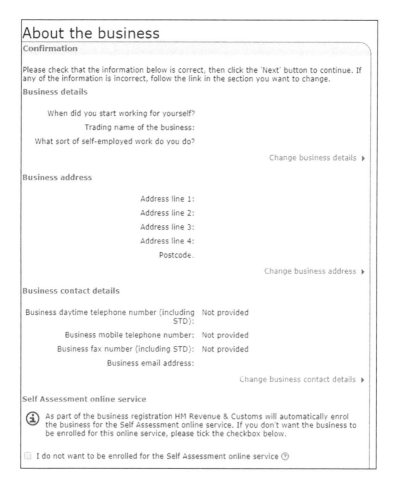

Having reviewed the data, click "Next" to get to the final stages. Woo hoo!

HMRC ask you to confirm that everything you think is correct is on there. You are confirming that you have registered as self-employed or a sole trader, and you get to pay income tax via self-assessment, and Class 2 National Insurance.

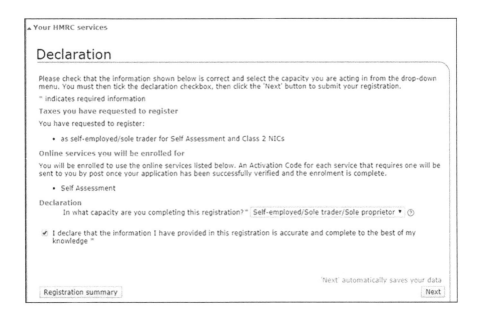

You are now enrolled for self-assessment and you are signing it as yourself, so you are the self-employed person. You tick the box; this is the one you do tick. You tick the box to declare that everything is correct to the best of your knowledge and then you click "Next".

Your HMRC services

Acknowledgment

> ✓ Your registration application was successfully submitted at

Acknowledgment reference:

Please note: The information you have submitted will now be verified. The security checks that HM Revenue and Customs (HMRC) perform mean that in most cases it will take approximately a week for this process to be completed but sometimes it may take longer.

Once your registration has been successfully verified HMRC will contact you separately about each tax you have registered for. This will be by post except for most VAT applications which will use the customer communications service. You can access customer communications from the 'Your HMRC services' page.

VAT communications relating to Transfers of a Going Concern or Changes of Legal Entity will be sent by post.

If you feel you need support or have questions to ask about specific topics, we recommend that you attend one of our live webinars. Follow the links below for more information and a list of the topics covered:

About HMRC's 'webinars'

Webinar Topics

HMRC recommend you print this information for your records by following the 'View and print' link below. Once you leave this page the information will no longer be available.

Save this page with your User ID and password. Then, if you receive an Activation Code from the Government Gateway, log in at HM Revenue & Customs to activate your online service.

View and print ▶

Further information

From the 2015 to 2016 tax year, Class 2 National Insurance contributions are collected through your Self Assessment Return and form part of the balancing charge that is due for payment by 31 January following the end of the tax year. For more information about paying Class 2 National Insurance contributions voluntarily if your profits are low, go to Voluntary National Insurance.

If you work as a subcontractor under the Construction Industry Scheme (CIS) you must register with HMRC before you start working.

If you are starting up in business and need more information follow the link Setting up.

Alternatively, to find out more about the help and support HMRC provide to business customers follow these links on GOV.UK:
Business and self-employed
Business support helpline

Log out and go to the HMRC homepage ▶
Go to Your HMRC services ▶

And that's it. You are done. You will see at the top you will get a time and date of when you submitted your application form and there will be a reference number in here as well. My advice to you would be to print this page. Either print it and put it into the folder that you've already now got your user id number in, or save it to your hard drive or your phone etc so that you can get back to it because they should complete all this work to set you up within 14 days and if you haven't heard within four to six weeks then you need to chase HMRC, quoting that acknowledgement reference number to find out what's happening.

What happens once you've registered for self-assessment?

Once you've registered for self-employment, HMRC will set up your records and send you a letter with a 10-digit reference, called a Unique Taxpayer Reference or UTR.

You should keep your Unique Taxpayer Reference in a safe place. HMRC say you should get the UTR within 10 days, but I have known it to take around four weeks to get this as it comes via post, but certain times of the year are really busy for them, so it has been known to take longer. Just make sure they always have your current address, as performers often move around the country depending on the work.

That is only the first stage. You will also get an activation code which has to be used within 28 days of the code being issued. That tends to mean 14 days as the letter can sit in an HMRC queue for a couple of days and then there can be postal delays. So as soon as you get the activation code, <u>use it</u>.

The process to do this is:

1. Log into your Government Gateway using the user name and password (that you hopefully printed and stored in your tax file) by going to www.gateway.gov.uk.

2. On the "Services" page, select the relevant service you want to activate (in this case self-assessment and self-employment).

3. Enter the activation code. Once accepted, you never need to use that code again and it can be destroyed. Just make sure you do have access to self-assessment before you destroy it, or add it to your tax file with the date you activated the account.

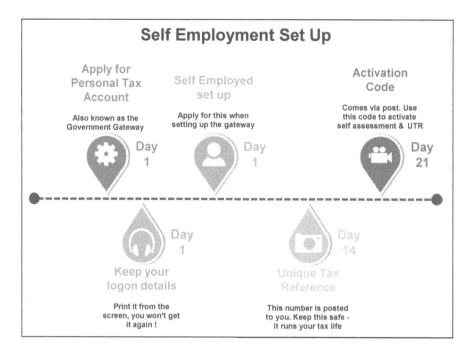

Sending your first tax return

You'll get a letter, usually in April or May, telling you when you need to send your first tax return. HMRC may get in touch earlier if you need to send a tax return back for a previous tax year. If you don't receive a letter or a tax return, you should contact HMRC.

How to complete the tax return is covered at a high level in Chapter 22; after all, I don't want to give away too much candy from my store.

Story:

A client came to me with a £1,500 penalty charge from HMRC (see the later chapter on penalties, Chapter 17).

She had been ignoring letters that she'd received from HMRC, as she thought she did not have to do a return as she was employed only on a PAYE basis for that tax year. In the end, she had debt collector notices and came to us for help.

It turned out that she had registered for self-employment as she was starting up on her own as of 1 April, not realising that five of these days fell into the prior tax year, so rightly the HMRC computer started to chase. A simple misunderstanding led to a lot of pain.

How was it resolved? We completed the self-assessment tax return for the year that was missing, stating that the business was started on 1 April, and put the year end to be 31 March the day before.

Her income, therefore, was £0, costs were £0, so there was no tax to pay. Then the client sent a grovelling letter to HMRC asking them to let her off the fine due to her "careless error".

The full £1,500 penalty was cancelled, but the original £100 late penalty was not refunded. I call that a win.

Things you need to do

☐ Register as self-employed.

☐ Keep a copy of your User ID.

☐ Make a note of your password (LastPass is a great tool).

☐ Activate your self-employment within 28 days.

If you need help with any of this, feel free to set up a call with us. Go to www.performanceaccountancy.youcanbook.me to find a time that's good for you.

CHAPTER 5:
Personal tax account

You often hear people talk about their personal tax account as well as the Government Gateway. Although they are different, they will eventually merge into the same thing for individuals. The personal digital tax account shows much more detail about you and your dealings with HMRC, plus it has the ability for HMRC to communicate with you.

You can do the following with this account:

- ♫ Check your income tax estimate and tax code.
- ♫ Fill in, send and view a personal tax return.
- ♫ Claim a tax refund.
- ♫ Check and manage your tax credits.
- ♫ Check your state pension.
- ♫ Track tax forms that you've submitted online.
- ♫ Check or update your marriage allowance.
- ♫ Tell HMRC about a change of address.
- ♫ Check or update benefits you get from work, for example company car details and medical insurance.

More services are being added, but it takes time.

In order to create the personal tax account, you can use this link: http://bit.ly/IdentitySA and this will allow you to create an account based on your Government Gateway, or via the system called "Verify" which verifies your ID. It does also give you the option to create an account from scratch, but the daft thing is that if you go to create the account, it only gives you the choice of setting up a Government Gateway account or via Verify. We do like little loops that go nowhere!

HMRC have produced a series of videos, and a quick one on the personal tax account can be found here http://bit.ly/PTA-Video.

The personal tax account does introduce 2-step verification, so be sure to register your mobile phone number and have it with you when you log on. If you change mobile numbers, then you will need to change the details held by HMRC or you won't be able to use your tax account.

Things you need to do

☐ If you registered for a Government
Gateway years ago, make sure you
get the "benefits" of the personal tax
account, as it shows your National
Insurance records, pension forecasts and
all sorts of fun.

CHAPTER 6:

What happens when you work abroad?

As musicians and singers develop in their career, more opportunities can be found in European orchestras and opera houses, so the lure of these organisations can be high. Whether it is a short-term contract for say one opera, or a whole season as chorus and cover, if your move abroad is not a permanent one, you need to complete the A1 form – but what is it?

This document shows employers, or promoters, that you are subject to the UK social security legislation for self-employment. So if you go abroad and do bits of work in the EU, the local social security deductions should not be taken from your fees. This also includes Switzerland.

You would normally pay National Insurance in the UK if you are usually (1) self-employed, or (2) working abroad temporarily for up to two years. You do need to keep this form safe and present it to the employer, but it will only be valid for the job you have applied for. If that is for a short season, for example on an opera, then it may only last for a couple of months, and then you have to reapply to HMRC for the next job. It is also country specific. Gone are the days of being able to apply for an A1 that will last for two years and covers all countries.

What are the benefits of an A1?

Well, the main benefit is that it removes the need to pay the local National Insurance or in-country social security, as you will be paying UK National Insurance. Any locally paid National Insurance is not actually an allowable expense for the UK tax return nor is it part of the foreign income tax deduction calculation.

However, the A1 does not remove the requirement for other local taxes, like the artist's tax, or local income tax. Local income tax (called withholding tax) is treated slightly different on the UK tax return, and it is declared separately in the foreign section as foreign income tax paid.

A common question at the moment is "How will this change after Brexit?" Well, if I had a crystal ball, I could tell you, but the simple answer at the moment is I have no idea. I don't think this has actually been scoped out yet, but European countries may come under the bilateral social security agreements. Time will tell, and obviously I'll update this section when we know more. Remember that you can register on my website for up-to-date information as I have it. Just go to the link below and complete the information on the right hand side.

https://performanceaccountancy.co.uk/contact-us/

What about the local income tax situation?

You often cannot escape local income tax in the country you perform in. They may deduct withholding tax which normally ranges from 15% to 30% and this can be hard to swallow when you also have to pay agent's commission and VAT from your own fees.

However, the withholding tax may not be lost. Providing you have a withholding tax certificate, if the amount deducted from your fee is 20% or less, and providing you are liable to pay UK income tax, the full amount may be offset against your UK income tax bill. But it does depend on having enough UK income tax to pay off. If you are deducted more than 20% withholding tax, then you can only offset 20% of the gross country income and the rest is lost. As said before, this is declared in the foreign section of the income tax return, and is covered in Chapter 14.

There is also something called the European Health Insurance Card, commonly known as EHIC, and an E111. If a person works in Europe, they can apply for an EHIC from the department of health, so you can get medical treatment if necessary, because of illness or accident in Europe. Forms are available from the Post Office (well if you can find a Post Office), or via https://www.nhs.uk/using-the-nhs/healthcare-abroad/.

So where do you get the A1 form to complete? Well, you can Google "A1 form" or "CA3837". This can only be completed online by either your employer or via your agent. However, I have known several singers that completed it themselves as though they were their own agent. This is often the case if you don't have an agent and you're just self-employed working through yourself.

Once completed, it can be automatically sent to HMRC, or printed and posted as usual. Don't expect a quick reply, as it can take around six to eight weeks, so always apply early. If you find you need another period, then a new form must be completed.

How to declare foreign income in your tax return, and the effect on self-employed income, is covered in Chapter 14.

Things you need to do

☐ Consider if you need an A1 form.

☐ Apply six weeks before taking up the contract.

☐ Obtain copies of the withholding tax certificate.

☐ Obtain the E111 form for health care.

CHAPTER 7:

Do you need an accountant?

Well that's a great question. When you first start up as self-employed, you may see the cost of an accountant as just that, a cost. You may think, "I can do this on my own. I don't need help. No, no, no. Yep. We can get it done. Let's save some money." However, if you don't start up correctly, bad habits creep in and then you may start losing track of things. You might start losing track of your receipts, losing track of sales invoices, forgetting to follow up with people. After all, how do you know the invoice you raised six months ago has been paid if you have no systems in place?

Accountants can be very useful. I say that sincerely folks (quoting Hughie Green). What a good accountant can do is take all of your bookkeeping from you and get it done quickly, more efficiently, especially with all these cloud computing software systems. Or indeed you could do your own bookkeeping with our tools and advice, and present us with the results, ready to do the tax return.

The main crux of using an accountant tends to be when it comes to your year end tax return. Do you know how to fill it in? Do you want to have a guess? Are you frightened of forms? There are certain rules that you can apply, but do you know what those rules are? You might decide that "Of course I can claim this entertainment of my agent because without my agent, I can't get any work, so I have to take them out for a meal", but if you claimed it, and then HMRC looked at your tax return and all the backing information, they're likely to fine you because that's not an allowable cost. Do you know the ins and outs of these rules? That's where an accountant that specialises in your area can be extremely useful. Why don't you talk to several, try and establish a relationship, and see what they can do for you?

Why change accountants if you already have one?

This can be an emotive topic depending on the relationship you have with your accountant and the number of years you have been together. People say it can be like a marriage: sometimes in harmony, and sometimes a few ructions are felt, with both of you needing to head towards the same goal of developing and growing your business. The accountant becomes fully versed in what your business does, where you are going and what you want to do to get there.

Like any other service or supply to your business, you should always ask yourself if you are getting good value for money out of your accountant. They can be a necessary item of expenditure for any business, but developing a relationship with them outside the yearly compliance role can enhance your business. Of course, they will be there if you just need compliance work and tax returns completed too.

I suggest you ask yourself the following questions:

- ♪ Am I getting value for money? – assuming you know the value you want.

- ♪ Does my accountant fully understand my business needs and what my plans are to grow the business in the future?

- ♪ Is the service satisfactory and are returns filed in good order and on time?

- ♪ Could I get better service elsewhere?

- ♪ Why has my accounting fee gone up?

- ♪ Has my business outgrown my accountant?

- ♪ Is my business treated like just another number to a large firm of accountants?

♪ Is the accountant moving with the times? With all the digital technology out there, are there better ways of doing things?

♪ Are they OK with technology and the way I want to move with it?

♪ Can they offer advice on my systems and processes to make me more efficient?

♪ Why do I only hear from them once a year? Surely things happen in the year that I need to be aware of?

When should you change accountants?

This is a question I'm often asked, and just before filing deadlines is not a good time, as you will be stressed, your current accountant may be stressed not knowing if they are helping you or not, and the new accountant will be fraught trying to get all the administration and agent bits through before they can work on your behalf. But sometimes we can work miracles. The impossible is harder.

I suggest you select a changeover date that is going to cause the least disruption in your business. The most obvious change date is the end of the business financial year. If you change mid-year, you may end up having additional catch-up fees as your new accountant needs to re-create what your old accountant has already done. This is especially true if your old accountant is also doing the bookkeeping for you.

Ensure all financial responsibilities to your accountant are discharged i.e. all outstanding bills have been paid.

And then – that's it – job done. Feel free to talk to us any time of the year if you are thinking of changing your accountant, or maybe getting an accountant, as you never know, new ideas may spark out of that conversation.

Here is my diary link. It's always best to book a call so I can be prepared and you'll get my fullest attention:
https://performanceaccountancy.youcanbook.me/

Lastly here's an infographic that can help you through the process.

SECTION 3:

How do I do all this?

CHAPTER 8:
What are bookkeeping records?

Whenever I take on a new client I always ask about their bookkeeping. Are they doing the bookkeeping or do they want us to do it for them? But sometimes there's a misunderstanding about what bookkeeping actually is. A fair enough question, as you don't set up as a musician or actor to do paperwork. If that is what you wanted to do, you'd be a bookkeeper or an accountant – dread the thought.

Sadly bookkeeping is a necessary evil, as you are now a business in your own right, and you need to stay on top of your business. It's just another thing that hits you after leaving college, but of course you could be self-employed whilst in college and juggling all your hats. Unfortunately being disorganised and putting paperwork off (or putting it in a box in the corner of your room) is just not a workable option. Of course, it is an option, as I have known people who have said to me that they didn't think they needed to do anything for the first five years after leaving college who have got one heck of a shock when they came onto HMRC's radar. Please don't go there, as it is an expensive mess to get yourself out of the big pile of brown sticky stuff. You are a grown-up now and you need to have an adult approach to this, and that means taking responsibility for your finances.

Being on top of your bookkeeping will help maintain a healthy cash flow and the knowledge that you may be able to afford the new Apple iPhone that you so desperately want. It can help you spot trends in your finances and also any potential financial problems before they become overwhelming.

Myth:

In my employed job, I always get tips in cash. I pocket them and don't need to put them on my tax return, and my employer does not add them to my payroll.

Fact:

Tips are a complicated area and I'm not going into it in detail in this book, but cash tips you receive from customers or out of a jar do need to be declared in your tax return. There is even a box for it in the employment section, so watch out if you work in an area where tips are commonplace.

Self-employed income and sales invoices

In its simplest form, bookkeeping is a list of your income and your expenditure. Your income is your self-employed income, be it invoices you have sent out and hopefully been paid for, remittances from your agent for any work, and student money if you're a teacher and people pay you. Technically you should be raising invoices, but I know a lot of people don't, so it will be a log of cash received or cheques received for your students, and any other type of performance income you might have had, be it from a profit share, etc. All of these should have some backing paperwork to equal what you have hopefully paid into a separate bank account for your self-employed business. The income does not include any PAYE work.

The actual record is a simple case of keeping a list, ideally in a spreadsheet, of all those income types with the amount and the date for the tax year (6 April to 5 April). You can actually do your accounts to 31 March; it doesn't make any difference.

Below is an example of what the income sheet would look like.

Date	Inv No	Sandy Clive Income list Customer	Service	Amount	Paid
23-Apr	24	Woodstock Orchestra	rehearsal	80.00	02-May
27-May	25	Cecelia Strings	rehearsal	50.00	28-May
24-Jun	26	Woking Bach society	Conducting	910.00	09-Jul
27-Jun	27	Harmonic choir	rehearsal	110.00	04-Jul
05-Jul	28	Oford Festival	rehearsal	140.00	25-Jul
11-Jul	29	Clifford Opera	Performance	110.00	16-Jul
11-Jul	30	Buckingham festival	Adjudication	110.00	
13-Sep	31	Jane Partridge	Lessons	100.00	19-Sep
13-Sep	32	Stuart Wilson	Lessons	100.00	19-Sep
13-Sep	33	Clive Janus	Lessons	100.00	19-Sep
13-Sep	34	Claire Smith	Lessons	100.00	20-Sep

Purchases and expenses

With expenses or costs you have incurred, it is exactly the same thing. You'll have receipts or purchases invoices made out to you, with detail values on them and not just a credit card receipt. You need to list those down, again ideally in a spreadsheet, categorise what the spend was for and then you can file the receipt away. Below is an example of how this sheet would work.

Date	Sandy Clive Income list Supplier	Details	Category	Gross Amount
02-Mar	Twitter	Advert	Marketing & Advertising	5.00
02-Mar	Easy Coffee	Coffee	Subsistence	1.00
02-Feb	Spotify	audio	Subscriptions	9.99
04-Mar	Academy Chimes	books	Books & other reference materials	39.58
10-Mar	MU Subs	MU	Subsistence	16.40
10-Mar	MAS	diary service	Phone & internet	84.00
16-Mar	Vodaphone	phone	Phone & internet	5.00
18-Mar	stringzone	strings	Repairs & Maintenance	35.60
22-Mar	Academy Chimes	books	Books & other reference materials	42.25
23-Mar	Smithzone	teaching room	Studio costs	150.00
23-Mar	Trainline	train ticket	Travel	32.25
24-Mar	Wix	Website	Marketing & Advertising	8.20
29-Mar	Boosey and Hawkes	books	Books & other reference materials	10.95
29-Mar	Music Jobs	Subscriptions	Subscriptions	30.00
30-Mar	Stringzone	strings	Repairs & Maintenance	18.80

Of course, there are apps available where you can take a photo of a receipt, or upload an invoice, and the app will read the information and turn that into data that will be downloaded into a spreadsheet so making analysis much easier with little manual input.

In the simplest form it's two spreadsheets effectively. You can also add in a mileage log if you are doing any miles in a car or on a bike for your self-employment, plus an additional sheet for evidence of phone costs and evidence of the hours worked at home for the working from home allowance.

Other records

For the working at home allowance, you will need to know how many hours you have worked each month from your home if you're going to be claiming any costs. You'll also need to keep copies of your utility bills, your rent, and your mortgage interest if you want to claim an actual cost of working from home. The methods of calculation are covered under the expenses section (Chapter 11). *The working from home allowance is only available to freelancers on a self-employed basis and not for directors of your own limited company, so just be aware of that difference if you do operate through a limited company.* There is something similar for directors.

You should have a record of any capital items you've purchased so it could be a piano or other new or secondhand instruments, a computer or Mac (I know how much actors and musicians love their Apple products) or potentially equipment for a voiceover studio. Even ball gowns or clothing for performances – that might cost quite a bit of money and can be used over a number of years – could be treated as capital, although most of the time they are expensed in the year of purchase.

Once you have identified capital costs, you can claim a capital allowance which is covered in Chapter 15. However, the spend will be incorporated in the costs spreadsheet, but just treated differently when it comes to the tax return.

So in simplest terms, having a spreadsheet consisting of a list of all your expenses categorised into what it is, a list of all your income, a mileage log and ideally some form of recording of the amount of time you spend in your home on your self-employed business will help.

Bank accounts

Something to seriously consider is to have a separate bank account for your self-employed business, which is where all your self-employed income goes, and all your self-employed costs come from. Keep it separate from what you may call your "life" account which manages things like rent, electricity, supermarket shop, going out, birthday presents, etc. If you have a PAYE job alongside your self-employed income, that is where your salary would go.

A sole trader/self-employed person is not legally separate from their business, so a separate bank account(s) is not a legal requirement; it just keeps your accounts clean and separates business and personal costs. Of course, if all your income is from self-employment, you will need to make transfers into your life account to keep your life running. You do need to check the bank terms and conditions as they may not allow a sole trader to run a personal account for their business transactions, and you may have to set up a sole trader account which will be subject to bank charges. This is particularly the case for NatWest and RBS.

Always spend time checking your bank statement each month, as there are always cases where you pay for things by direct debit, and you forget to put it on your costs sheet, for example, Equity or MU membership. There is always the possibility of fraud or just genuine mistakes in the bank. How often do you sit there puzzled by a charge you can't recognise, or think "I must cancel this subscription to xyz" but forget as it's only a small amount? Well, those small amounts add up.

Now what?

Chapter 13 looks at whether you need to use an accounting system for your records, but we do provide an Excel template for people to use when they come on board as clients that they can use, especially if they're not sure of what records to keep.

I do stress the importance of having things electronically in a spreadsheet like Excel, although you can keep details in a manual cash book. They still exist in good stationery stores. But if you do this and use an accountant, it may increase the bill, as they will need to convert the data into electronic form in order to work on it efficiently, and in the near future, records will need to be kept electronically.

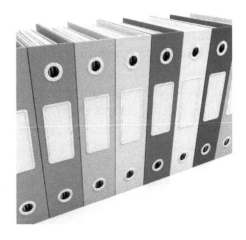

HMRC are not prescriptive at the moment about the format of records your business should keep so the above is all pretty good guidance for starting out. But things are changing as I've already hinted.

One question I'm often asked is: How long must I keep the bookkeeping records for? You need to keep records for six years plus the tax year we are in, so effectively this ends up being seven years.

Some transactions might span several years, for example the spend on a new instrument. If they do, you need to keep the paperwork from when that item first came into use. Let's say you've bought a harp, it's been depreciating over 20 years, so you'll need to keep the financial record of that purchase of the harp even though it's 20 years old. As we may (or may not) know, some instruments don't necessarily lose value, so you may be keeping that receipt for quite a while. It's always quite a task going back through endless records to find out what makes a capital allowance pool as often people just have balance brought forward from last year. If possible – DON'T. Keep your detailed list of capital item purchases, and when you disposed of them, as it makes things so much easier in the future. Trust me.

Now, as HMRC do start compliance checks into tax returns so if they find anything that looks a bit ooh-ooh, then they could in theory go back even further. I thoroughly promote the idea of being able to scan receipts and things onto a hard drive. As long as it's readable, printable and you can get at it, then that should be adequate for your accounting records. But both sides of the piece of paper in theory have to be scanned. So if there's something on the back page you need to make sure that that is also scanned in. I know – it is a pain. I invested in a really nifty bit of kit called ScanSnap ix500 which automatically scans double-sided papers and is so quick and takes up very little space. It's the best thing I've purchased for my business in years!

It is worth noting that a lot of receipts are on thermal paper and the writing disappears after six months or quicker if in the sunlight, so take a copy of the receipt or even a photocopy on an old-fashioned machine. Oh, heaven forbid, you may have one lurking around.

Of course there's always the possibility of losing your records. That's a bit of a problem because if you can't replace them, as they've been lost, stolen or destroyed, you need to find some way to re-create them. And if you can't, you need to tell HMRC self-assessment department straight away. Unfortunately, they don't take too kindly as they always think you should be backing things up, especially if you've got it on a hard drive and the hard drives got corrupted. What can happen is they can open an investigation into your tax return and if you don't have adequate support and receipts to back things up, they will disallow the claim. So if you don't have back-up for something big, potentially that can lead to a whole new amount of tax, National Insurance and student loan having to be paid.

Keep your paperwork organised and referenced, and things will be a doddle. Of course, you could hire a bookkeeper or accountant to help you or just as a consult for getting going. They may know little hints and tips that you didn't realise, or suggest you don't claim things that may land you in trouble.

Story:

Sometimes it is really hard to find the time to do your bookkeeping, and I really understand that. However, I had one client full of reasons not to do it:

April – Too early in the tax year to do anything

May – Oh, it's my birthday month, and to do this would cause a downer on my month

June – Nope – Son's birthday month and ditto May

July and August – It's the summer holidays. No, not this month as I need to spend all my time with my son

September – Oh I've let the business slide a bit over the summer so need to catch up

October – But it's Halloween and ditto May

November – Err, I'll think of something

December – But it's Christmas and it would cause a downer for the month

January – Oh can you do it all for me??

This client frequently filed late and did not mind the £100 as she had nothing stopping her in February and March.

The moral of the story is don't put off doing your tax return and instead do things as you go. Can you really not find half an hour a week to enter data into a spreadsheet or manual cash book, and file your receipts neatly in a file?

Just think of the stress you will feel when spending days on end catching up with the year. Can you remember what you purchased from Boots and if it was personal or business spend? Why waste £100? What else could it buy you?

Things you need to do

- ☐ Obtain an expanding January to December file to keep receipts in.

- ☐ Consider a lever arch file for bank statement, invoices, payslips/remittances.

- ☐ Get a stamper with "paid" on it so you can stamp each physical invoice you have paid or been paid.

- ☐ Consider the use of Excel or an accounting or receipt collection software.

- ☐ Allocate half an hour a week to keep everything up to date and tidy.

- ☐ Label each folder as you need to keep the records for six+ years.

CHAPTER 9:

Cash accounting method – what is it?

This is a question that gets asked a lot, because there is a box in the self-assessment tax return that asks whether you have used cash accounting to do your self-assessment and your self-employed accounts. Cash accounting is exactly what it says on the tin. It says you make your accounting records when you physically receive payment into your business. It doesn't matter if it's received via PayPal, received directly into a bank account, received physically in cash or cheque. It's when you have received the actual money.

Let's say for example, you raise an invoice to Mr. and Mrs. Blythe for their daughter's singing lessons. You raise it at the beginning of the term, but you don't actually get paid it until near the end of the term. You would only account for that invoice when you received the money from Mr. and Mrs. Blythe. You don't account for the invoice when it's raised.

Equally, on the other side, you account for your costs when you have physically paid for them. That is very easy if you actually pay in cash, by direct debit or transfer out of your bank account, or indeed if you pay via PayPal, because they're fairly instant payment methods. The tricky bit comes if you pay by credit card: you might have put the cost on a credit card but you haven't actually paid for it until you pay the credit card bill. If you only pay a credit card bill a certain amount per month, it's very hard to know whether you've paid for which business expense. That's what cash accounting is.

There are problems with using cash accounting. You have to keep very good records to know when you have physically paid for things, but if you make a loss in your business, then you cannot do anything with that loss. It could be your first year of business so you've had a lot of set-up costs, not too many people know about you, so they haven't employed you very much, but that loss is dead, so you cannot carry it forward to next year to use the loss against any profit in the following year. You also cannot offset it against any other income in that tax year like PAYE to get any rebate.

It also means if you have purchased any capital items, a new instrument, a computer, an expensive printer, or various things like that, under the cash accounting rules, it is a cost incurred at that time, because you've paid for it at that time, and therefore it goes into the accounts for that tax year. That means you cannot claim any capital allowances. All costs come out of that year. Again, if you make a loss, you cannot carry forward that loss or the capital cost into next year. The only positive side of that is if you're buying a new instrument on a loan agreement, then technically you're only putting towards let's say £100 a month, instead of £3,000 for the instrument. You'd actually expense £100 a month for it.

HMRC seem to be wearing two different hats. They say you have to have the invoices and receipts to be able to do proper accounting, but then under making tax digital (due to come in some time after April 2020), they're encouraging people just to do their accounts from bank statements. They want their cake and they want to eat it.

Now, on the other side is **accrual accounting**. This is the recognised form of accounting that accountants will use all the time, and it is definitely our method of doing accounts. This is when the invoice is accounted for when it is raised. Throughout this book, we use accrual accounting.

Let's go back to Mr. and Mrs. Blythe. As before, you invoiced them at the beginning of the term, which is January, but they didn't pay you until the end of April, which is the end of the school term. However, you would account for the income in January, and you ignore when they actually paid the bill, which may be a little harsh because it is across two tax years. By the time you actually have to pay the tax on that payment, they should have already paid you. The good thing about the accruals method for purchases is that you base your bookkeeping record on the supplier invoice date. Even though you might not pay it until two weeks later, two months later, six months later, you account for it at the time you incur the cost, at the time the liability hits you, really.

There are various accounting rules we can jiggle around with. If you've taken a deposit upfront for a wedding, but the wedding is not until four months' time, then you can defer that to match the income off with the costs. That gets a bit complicated. Accountants can easily do it. It's what we're trained to do.

Other good things about accrual accounting are that you can claim capital allowances and put off the costs of items until later years, and if you do incur losses, you are able to carry them forward for future years or offset them against other income.

Beware, if you are a limited company, the cash accounting system is not open to you. You can do cash accounting for VAT, that's a completely separate thing, but actually to run your accounts and your corporation tax, you cannot use cash accounting. Many people do, because they don't understand the difference. Several people will do cash accounting throughout the year and their accountant will then pull it back into line to say, "It has to be under an accrual basis." Cash accounting is really only open to the self-employed.

That's it. Never tick the "Have you used a cash basis?" on the self-assessment tax return if you are doing the accruals basis, or if you're doing the cash basis, make sure you understand its drawbacks.

Story:

One of our musician clients came to me with cash records. I asked him about how he came to calculate income and as expected it was based on cash he made a note of and money into his bank. I asked him how he knew if everybody had paid him. Blank look!

A couple of weeks later he returned to me to say that he was missing payments for work done seven months before. He now keeps records of invoices raised and notes when the payment is received. Result – £1,500 more cash in his bank and a much better idea on cash flow and where he is financially wise.

CHAPTER 10:

What should be on my invoice?

An invoice is a document that shows what work has been done (or items sold), the amount that the customer or client owes you, and when and how they should pay you. Normally there would be an agreement of when an invoice should be sent which may be after work has been completed, payment in advance, or at staged payments throughout the process.

Many clients get invoicing, not necessarily wrong, but slightly incorrect when they start out. If this carries on for a while and if you end up being VAT registered, these bad habits continue. Although there are no hard and fast rules in law as to what should be on an invoice, there are requirements per VAT law, so the following is based on those regulations.

To keep good records, you should raise an invoice for each piece of self-employed work. It may be the case that your agent provides you with a self-billing invoice, which is perfectly acceptable. Remember to add it to your sales listing. An invoice does not have to be in paper format and can be an electronic invoice.

The invoice that you issue to a customer should show the following:

♪ An invoice number that is UNIQUE and follows on from the number of the previous invoice even if you cancel or "spoil" an invoice number.

♪ Your name or trading name and address (if you are a company, you need to also show the company number and the registered office address).

♪ Your contact details in case the client/customer needs to get hold of you.

♪ Your customer's name or trading name and address.

♪ Invoice date (and a tax point date if different from the invoice date). I will go into that shortly.

♪ The description of what has been sold or supplied or the service performed.

♪ The rate of any cash discount.

Here is an example of an invoice.

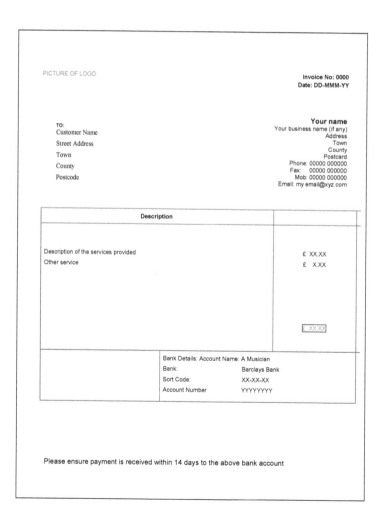

What is the issue about the invoice date i.e. the tax point?

The date of the invoice may not be the tax date of the supply. The tax point is the date that the sale is considered to be done. It may not be the date of the delivery of the goods or services, as payment in advance can be made as a deposit. Reporting is done based on the date of this invoice.

The date that the supply physically takes place for a sale of goods is the earlier of:

- ♪ When the supplier sends the goods to the customer;
- ♪ When the customer collects the goods from the supplier;
- ♪ When the goods are made available to the customer.

For services, it is based on the time that the service is carried out and completed, although it may not be invoiced.

I often get asked about invoices raised prior to the end of the tax year, but not paid for until after the start of the new tax year. Following the rules, if you have done the work, then it needs to be accounted for (and invoice raised) in the year you did the work, and put in the income list for that year, irrespective of when it was paid. Should a deposit invoice be raised in one year for a job in the following year, it is perfectly allowable to remove that invoice for the current year and allocate it to the following year so matching income with costs.

Of course, all this changes if you decide to use the cash basis, as you account for the invoices and income when the money is received, so an invoice raised this year not paid until next year will be accounted for next year.

Other things to consider

There are a few other things you may want to put on your invoice:

- ♪ Terms of business, so when you expect to be paid.
- ♪ Your bank details so people know how they can pay you.

♪ Some customers want to see the confirmation statement that you are responsible for your own tax and National Insurance, so they may ask that your unique tax reference number and National Insurance number is on your invoice.

You may wish to include something about terms and conditions, or the fact that you have the right to charge interest for late payments under the late payment act of 2013, but sometimes this can be overkill.

A quick note about the numbering of invoices: Always start at number 1 and continue the number range with nothing missing. Don't precede it with initials or anything that relates to a customer so invoice 1 you may say is AH001, and invoice 2 you may call KB001, but HMRC does not know if you are missing any invoices between AH and KB, and you have no way of proving it. Just do 001, 002 etc.

Things you need to do

☐ Have an invoicing system in place, be it some kind of app or a simple Word document (make sure you keep copies of them all and don't just overtype).

☐ What are your terms and conditions? Are they clear and given to your customers, clients and students?

☐ Make sure your bank details are clear, and set up a separate bank account for your self-employed business.

☐ Have a numbering system that starts from 1, and nothing fussy with clients' initials at the front, or the month or anything strange like that.

CHAPTER 11:

Tax deductible expenses for actors, musicians and performers

Myth 1:
I've been told that HMRC pay back all my expenses, but I've not received anything yet.

Myth 2:
I've worked out my tax on my income, and now I have deducted my costs from the tax.

Fact:
HMRC do not give you back the money for your costs. The costs and expenses are taken off your income which is called profit, and then the tax and National Insurance charges are calculated after taking into account any allowances (if there is no other income).

Taxes and actors, musicians and other performing artists tend not to be a happy mix. Taxes and the administration of their business is often the last of their concerns but can be the first thing on their worry list. An artistic temperament simply does not interface well with the exacting rule-filled world of accounting and HMRC. Many performers tend to avoid the situation and consequently leave themselves faced with the panic filing of tax returns, bad advice or just not filing their tax returns at all.

A professional performer needs to keep proper accounting records as these contain the information required for tax returns. HMRC can request to inspect records so it is best to keep up to date with it all on an ongoing basis rather than just throwing it at somebody a few days before the deadline. These records should include the details of expenses incurred that are tax deductible. (Keeping proper accounting records is covered in Chapter 8 – if you skipped over it for some reason.)

The law states that expenses claimed are to be "wholly and exclusively incurred in the performance of the business", but it is not always so clear-cut. Many items of expenditure could be claimed as "wholly and exclusively", but this should be used with care and not abused. Over claiming can lead to problems later if there is an inspection by the tax man and keeping paperwork is key to supporting any claims.

I have written this chapter so that you can see at a glance which expenses should be allowable for your self-assessment. The information is a guide only as situations can vary and tax rules often change.

Agents and promotion

Agent fees and commission

Should you use an agent to get bookings, they will charge an agreed commission or fee and, most likely, VAT. These costs are allowable as a tax deduction.

VAT can also be reclaimed if you are standard rate VAT registered, depending on your VAT status, or treated as a cost in full if you are not VAT registered or flat rate VAT registered – VAT is covered in Chapter 19. People often begrudge paying agent fees, but without the agent, how likely would you be to have got the job?

Subscriptions to trade journals and websites (e.g. *The Stage*, Casting Call Pro, Singers Pro)

These are subscriptions that enable you to keep up to date with happenings in your industry and also can assist you in finding work. These publications are often the only source of audition opportunities, especially if you do not have an agent. These costs are allowed as a tax deduction.

Trade union membership and casting resource listings (e.g. Equity, Spotlight, Musicians' Union)

Although it's not compulsory to join one of these organisations, the purpose of them is to assist you in your career. Some organisations offer insurance, which can save on your outgoings. The photography cost for the headshots needed for some organisations (e.g. Spotlight) is tax deductible (see below).

Marketing

Every performer needs to invest in self-marketing. Essential marketing costs that are tax deductible include your Spotlight annual fee and any subscriptions to casting websites like Constant Casting, Casting Call Pro and Starnow, as has been mentioned above.

Photography and showreel production and distribution

The cost of hiring a photographer and getting headshots and photographs is tax deductible, but usually the cost is spread over a couple of years, depending on how often you update your portfolio. The cost of creating a voiceover CD or showreel should also be tax deductible and this cost is also usually spread over three years.

Don't forget that the cost of make-up and haircuts, which are needed specifically for photo shoots, film premieres or promotional events, should also be deductible (more on these costs later).

Public relations

If you are lucky enough to have a PR manager, their costs are classed as marketing and are also allowed as a business expense.

Website and website management fees

If you design a website to promote yourself as a performer, or hire a designer to do it for you, any fees and annual domain registrations, ongoing maintenance or monthly subscription costs are tax deductible. Upfront design costs are not immediately tax deductible as generally the design lasts more than one year, and the cost should be spread over that period.

Recordings of own performances to use as marketing and advertising material

This is another form of marketing cost that is allowable. It includes the costs associated with the production and distribution of a showreel. Please be aware that the sale of recordings is very different as the correct licences need to be obtained to be able to do this for copyright reasons and manufacturing. Once obtained, the licences are an allowable cost, with sales treated as taxable income and any costs incurred are allowable costs of sales. However, if any of the recordings are used for personal use, the appropriate proportion of cost must be disallowed.

Entries to networking events

Networking is often a way that you make contacts, for example, The Voiceover Network and Reading Arts Business Club. It needs to be appropriate for your business. Performing is your business and needs to be treated as such. You should be able to claim the entry costs into events and the travel costs to get there. Again, consider any duality. If you plan to travel to Cardiff to go to a networking event for Welsh actors and plan to visit friends and family at the same time, then there is a duality and the travel aspect would not be an allowable tax deduction (see more on travel below).

Research and training

Theatre, concert, gallery and museum tickets

A performer is often expected to research their roles or possible roles and the accepted way of doing this is by attending performances, and visiting galleries and museums in order to get a flavour of roles that may be auditioned. This should be used with caution as attending a Robbie Williams concert is not going to be accepted as research for somebody preparing for Henry V, however, it may be appropriate for a lighting designer to see the use of lasers in a different environment. It all comes down to being "wholly and necessary" for your business. You can also claim the travel and mileage allowance to get to the research place (more on that later).

DVDs, CDs, cinema and movie subscriptions

This is also an area of expenditure that can be allowable for performers who work in the appropriate field. As with the theatre section above, it needs to be related to what you do. An opera singer can buy DVDs and CDs that relate to roles they may study. Again, sense prevails. It would not be deemed as business for a baritone singer to buy a CD of soprano arias. In some cases, the TV licence and satellite or cable subscription can be allowable business expenses for some professions, for example, movie actors, directors and journalists.

Training, workshops and classes, singing and dancing lessons

It is vital that any performer continues with training and upkeep of their skills. The cost of attending regular acting classes, workshops, movement or dance classes, vocal coaching, music lessons etc, should be tax deductible. If you are a musical actor and have a singing or voice tutor, then these costs should also be allowable. Even the cost of attending a full-time filming or Shakespearian course should be deductible.

It is all about updating and enhancing skills to keep you employable and noticed. However, it is not about acquiring

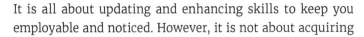

new skills that are unrelated to your current business, for example training to be a plumber, as these are regarded as capital in nature and in effect a new business. A new skill can be close to your current profession but may be non-tax deductible, for example, an actor may choose to develop circus skills in order to market them as a new skill. However, if circus skills were needed for a role already landed, then it would be an allowable cost.

Business and marketing training

In order to enhance marketing and business skills it is often appropriate to undertake training that is not directly part of your skills, for example, an online course on how to build videos that can be used to promote your performances, social media advertising, website building, bookkeeping courses. These would be allowable expenses. All of these help to build a more rounded businessperson, or help to highlight areas where outsourcing could be appropriate. After all, if you don't have some understanding of the basics, how can you instruct others to do their best for you?

Outfits and equipment required for performance

Performance wear or costumes

Clothing is always an area that gets high attention. The rule is that clothing is not allowed unless purchased for work during a film, TV or stage performance. If items of clothing and footwear are purchased specifically for a role, the costs can be deducted for tax purposes as long as they are unlikely to be used for any other purpose. Clothing for rehearsal purposes is not tax allowable as it has a duality of benefit. Duality is when an item can be used for a non-business purpose as well as a business purpose. We need clothes to protect our modesty and give us warmth!

Myth:

I can claim all my clothes that I purchase, because as an actress I have to look good for my public.

Fact:

NO NO NO NO NO. I think that sums it up.

It is the same for musicians. If concert dresses or opera gowns are purchased specifically to perform in, then they are allowable. However, if the performer wears the clothing to the venue and back home again, there is a duality so therefore it becomes non-allowable. HMRC are very hot on this area and there have been investigations into people where this type of expense has been higher than expected. If you can get a photo of yourself wearing the clothing in the setting for which it was purchased it helps as back-up should the need arise, for example, that new outfit for the red carpet you had to attend or the medieval costume you had to provide for a production of Romeo and Juliet.

The same rules apply to a dancer. Dance shoes should be a fully allowable business expenditure as, without these, you are unable to carry out your business. There is unlikely to be a duality of benefit as the shoes are highly specialised.
You are not going to wear your pointe shoes to the supermarket! As above, dancewear for auditions and rehearsals is not tax deductible. By all means show it as a cost to the business, but that will be a difference between your own accounts and your tax accounts.

If you are reimbursed for any costumes or performance outfits, this reimbursement must be included as income.

Costume cleaning

Once an item of clothing has been deemed a costume and allowable, any professional cleaning of the item can be claimed. What you will not be able to claim is the box of washing powder used to wash your clothes. You will still need to keep receipts from the drycleaner. If you are reimbursed for any cleaning, then this reimbursement must be included as income.

Props

These are also a business expense when used in a production environment, be it theatre, concert, workshop and so on, provided there is no dual use of the item. An upright candelabra looks great to set a stage for a concert but if it then returns home and is used in a personal environment it becomes a dual benefit item and is not allowable.

Clothes can also be used as props or in workshops. The same applies with regards to duality. The best advice again is to keep a detailed record of what is being claimed as props and when used, and ideally photographic evidence of their use. A size 10 person purchasing size 18 clothes for props in a workshop can probably get away with them as expenses, but then it comes down to detailed records being maintained.

Strictly speaking, props tend to last longer than one year and should be treated as capital items and there are separate rules for capital items. Please see Chapter 15 for more details. Generally the costs of these items are spread over their expected useful life, although an annual investment allowance is given for capital costs but that amount varies each year. It is always best to seek advice.

Hairdressing, make-up and wigs

Myth:
I want to claim all my hairdressing costs and make-up, because I have to look good for my public and to carry on looking like my headshot.

Fact:
Err, no again. Try having headshots that represent you and not you after several hours at the hairdresser and time with the make-up artist. Everyday grooming is not allowable.

Wigs and accessories for the purpose of performances are allowed as tax deductions. This is particularly useful for people who work in period dramas or as pantomime dames. Cleaning costs of wigs is also an allowable expense. As before, if there is any reimbursement for cleaning this reimbursement must be included as income.

Over the last few years HMRC has taken a hard line on hairdressing and make-up costs. General recurring hairdressing is not an allowable tax expense. However, an allowance for specific events, performances and concerts can be claimed. Stage and TV make-up can be taken as a tax deduction, but day-to-day make-up would be harder to justify.

Contact lenses

If you normally wear spectacles but the character you are playing doesn't wear glasses, you will have to purchase and wear contact lenses, and these expenses should be deductible. However, you need to consider duality of benefit. If you wear the contact lenses for any other purpose other than performing, they will not be allowable. This includes while travelling to and from engagements.

Instrument maintenance

The costs of hiring, repairing, maintaining and insuring instruments are deductible expenses. However, if the instruments are used in a PAYE employment there needs to be a reduction in the amount being claimed as the costs are not wholly for your self-employed business. The PAYE code applied to the salaried work should include an allowance for these expenses and therefore this would be a double deduction which would not be allowed. If there is no allowance in the PAYE coding, an application can be done to HMRC via the helpline, or the costs can be put through on the tax return in the employment section.

Play texts, books, biographies, scores, downloaded music and backing tracks

This is often a big area of expenditure. Provided it is used for business purposes then these costs are allowable. As above, a baritone purchasing a sheet music book of soprano arias would not be an appropriate cost unless he sang with a soprano as a duo, ran workshops for singers, or needed to build a library for pupils. It relates to what would be acceptable for your business. The same is true for play texts for actors.

Travel expenditure

Travel to and from auditions and performances

Most travelling costs incurred for acting, dancing, and performing-related activities are tax deductible. This includes travel from home to audition, rehearsals and performance venues, and research trips. These costs are normally train, tube, bus or taxi fares, as well as mileage and reasonable subsistence costs, which are both explained later.

Oyster card costs are tax allowable for journeys. Transport for London weekly travel summary emails that show each trip can be used for your accounting records.

Travel costs for overseas work (auditions or performances) can also be claimed, be it air, boat or train fares, as well as related expenses such as accommodation costs (see below). However, there are complex rules if family accompany you or if there is a holiday element to the trip. Specific advice needs to be sought if this is the case.

Subsistence – food and drink

The cost of meals is not normally an allowable business expense as there is a duality of benefit – we all have to eat therefore it fails the "wholly" test. However, where travel costs have been incurred it is normally allowed to claim reasonable expenses on food and drink if the business trip is outside the normal pattern of travel. Food expenses incurred on trips to the normal base of work, for example a school where you are a tutor or an orchestral rehearsal venue, would be disallowed. Expenses incurred for one-off engagements would be allowable, as well as costs of being on tour or filming away from home. Generally speaking, it is not allowable if it is within 10 miles of your base location. Always consider what the "reasonable man" would expect as allowable.

It is always best to have a receipt for your meal, but this may not always be possible, especially if you are in a group of people and you pay your share. A contemporary record like a diary or cashbook entry could be used to support the claim for small amounts. Just remember to keep your diary.

Alcohol is always asked about. If your normal routine is to have a glass of wine with your evening meal when at home then it is reasonable to allow a glass of wine with your meal when you are travelling.

Some performers get paid a per diem for food and beverages whilst on tour. As part of self-employment this allowance needs to be declared as income, and then the actual costs incurred treated as expenses. Of course, it you don't spend all the per diem, you make a profit that is taxable.

Questions always arise with regards to whether the costs for buying your agent, a business contact or prospective clients a drink or meal are tax deductible. The answer is no. This is entertaining (unless the person is your paid employee) and the costs involved are specifically disallowed by law. If you insist on paying, obtain two separate checks and pay for both but only claim your own costs. In your own accounts you can put through both costs to recognise the cost of running your business, but you will have a difference between your own management accounts and tax accounts.

Hotel expenses

Performers often have to stay away from home in various types of accommodation, especially if on tour, filming on location and even if they are promoting themselves in a different area of the country or world. The whole hotel bill would generally be allowable including meals, but sundry items such as the bar bill and newspapers should not be claimed.

Don't forget there are complex rules if family accompanies you or if there is a holiday element to the trip. Specific advice needs to be sought if this is the case.

Motor expenses

This is always a minefield. Actual costs of running a car for business can be put through as business costs in a proportion of business use versus personal use. The cost of the car is not included in this calculation but costs that can be included are car insurance, car recovery, road fund licence, valet services, MOT, servicing, repair, fuel, oil, replacement blades, and so on. A mileage log needs to be kept to establish how much the vehicle is used for business. The total cost for the year is divided by the business mileage for the year, and that is the allowable expense. Alternatively, a mileage allowance can be claimed.

Mileage

A detailed mileage log needs to be kept showing all business trips made. However, a simpler method would be to keep a diary with addresses and postcodes of where you are travelling from and to, and then at the end of the day, week or month, work out the mileage. The allowance below is then applied to the mileage. The rate used depends on the mode of transport, if there are any business passengers, and the number of business miles done in the year.

Rate per mile	Car / van	Motor cycle	Bicycle
Business miles up to 10,000	45p	24p	20p
Business miles over to 10,000	25p	24p	20p

I have put the bicycle mileage in here, but this is only ever mentioned as an allowable cost for employees (i.e. what the employer can pay the employee for using their bike), but there is no mention of this anywhere for simplified expenses for the self-employed. That does not seem fair, does it? HMRC want to treat employees and self-employed the same, but you get a different answer from different inspectors on this. So at the moment, I say claim the 20p a mile from using your bike. I can't see you transporting a full-sized harp on the bike unless you have one of those cargo bike trailers. Just don't hit any potholes.

An additional 5p a mile can be claimed for each business passenger, as long as they are an employee or fellow director.

There can be no duality of purpose for the business trip. For example, you may attend a conference in Staffordshire but if you take the family so they can enjoy Alton Towers, the conference cost will be allowable but not the travel to get there.

It needs to be made clear that journeys to and from PAYE jobs are not business trips and therefore must not be aggregated with freelance business miles. This is classed as "ordinary commuting" and there is no tax relief on this.

Office equipment and costs

Premises costs

If you hire space in an arts centre or have your own studio space outside the home, you can charge the business for these costs. If you have built or purchased a building for your business, you cannot claim the costs of this and there are other rules that apply. The lease of business premises normally means you are responsible for utility costs (electricity, gas), maintenance (cleaning, repairs) and the rent or lease costs. Should you work from home, there are other rules to be applied.

Many musicians teach in a school on a freelance basis and have to pay a room rent to carry out the teaching. This can also be deducted as an allowable cost.

Working from home

Most performers use their home for acting, music practice and related activities including researching roles, browsing for castings, telephoning and emailing agents, learning scripts and practising their art. There is an allowance for using your home as your work place and it is given if you don't have other options for working. It can be as little as a desk in the corner for paperwork, to a dedicated room. There are two options when dealing with working from home costs:

1. Work out the total spend of running the home. This includes mortgage interest, council tax, house insurance, gas, electricity (not water), cleaning and repairs/redecoration to the business room. If a room is dedicated to the business, divide the yearly total running cost by the number of rooms (minus the kitchen and bathrooms) and multiply by the number of rooms used by the business. If the room is not solely dedicated to the business, this figure needs to be reduced proportionately. If a room is dedicated to the business and you claim 100% of one room, this can have a knock-on effect for capital gains tax when you sell the property and potentially business rates and revised mortgages.

2. There is a standard amount that can be claimed and accepted by HMRC. Up to 2012/2013, the amount was £4 per week. However, this has now changed and is based on amount of time spent in the business room. Evidence needs to be kept by logging the number of hours and then the allowance taken. Current rates are:

Less than 25 hours per month	£0
25 – 50 hours per month	£10
51 – 100 hours per month	£18
101+ hours per month	£26

If the standard amount per month is chosen, it needs to be consistent through the years and only changed where there is a significant change of circumstances.

iPads, electronic notebooks, computers, printers, camera

These types of cost are known as capital items, i.e. they would normally have a life of more than one year. These are still allowable as business costs, but they are in the special category of capital and you obtain an allowance for their cost. Generally, the costs of these items are spread over their expected useful life, however, the government does allow an investment allowance, which would normally cover the cost of these items in their first year. There may be personal use for these assets, in which case the allowance is restricted to the amount of business use only. If you are unsure, it is best to contact an accountant for help.

Computer software and security

On the assumption that the computer is used for business, any business-based software can be treated as a tax deductible. This would include products such as Microsoft Office, internet security, Sibelius, notation software, publishing tools, accounting software etc. However, if the computer is for personal and business use, the costs of the software used would have to be apportioned between business and personal unless the software is entirely business specific. Details should be kept on usage and the proportion allocated each year. If personal use is incidental, it is likely that the whole cost can be taken as an allowable expense.

Ink, stationery and mailing costs

These generally are all allowable as a deduction for tax purposes if for business use. The birthday card and postage to Auntie Flo would not count, however thank you cards to your agent and suchlike would be allowable. Royal Mail Online do a prepaid postage account. The cost to put money in that account would not be a tax deductible, but each time you dipped into it to mail anything related to your business would be, so print the confirmation email of the evidence of spend.

Phone and internet costs

Technically, it is the actual cost of calls that can be claimed but many people who run their own business have all-encompassing packages for unlimited calls and unmetered broadband. If there has been no increase in costs of phone packages and broadband, then no costs can be attributed to the business. However, most businesses allocate a proportion of the costs to the business. Empirical evidence needs to be maintained to justify the amount allocated.

Accountancy, banking and legal costs

Accounting and bookkeeping fees

On the whole, these costs are allowable. There are of course exceptions. They mainly include any fees payable for completing tax returns and the set-up costs of forming a company. If the accountant's bill is all-inclusive, request a breakdown so allowable costs can be included as a deduction.

As a self-employed person, you have to play Class 2 National Insurance. This is classed as a personal cost and is therefore not an allowable business expense.

Bank account/overdraft charges

As I mentioned earlier, I advise having a separate bank account for your performing business. That way any finance costs in running the account truly belong to the business and are not due to general living costs being taken from earnings. The financing costs are an allowable tax deduction. Monthly charges applied to a business bank account are allowable.

If you only have one bank account, then the financing costs will not be able to be claimed as it is not possible to distinguish between interest charged on the business and personal expenditure. The same applies to bank charges.

Legal and professional fees

On the whole, these costs are allowable. You cannot include costs in relation to the purchase of large items, settling tax disputes, fines for breaking the law and costs for creating or filing tax returns. Speeding tickets and parking fines are not allowable costs for business and tax. It is always best to ask advice before claiming legal and professional costs against your tax bill.

Employee costs

Employees

Should you employ somebody to work for you, the cost of their salary and employer's National Insurance, plus any other benefits you give them, is an allowable expense for the business. You need to be running a recognised payroll scheme and reporting monthly to HMRC. However, the cost of a nanny is not an allowable tax deduction as it is not a business expense. They may allow you to work, but it is not a direct cost of the business.

Employing relatives

Payments can be made to a non-earning spouse or other family member for secretarial services or suchlike, but the payment must be a wage considered appropriate for the amount of work that they undertake within the business. There needs to be an actual transfer of funds to the employee's own bank account for it to be an allowable deduction. The spouse or family member must still be on a recognised payroll scheme.

Although we have said that entertaining is not allowable, should you have employees, you are able to spend up to £150 per employee in the year on their entertaining as long as it is wholly and exclusively for the purposes of the trade and is not merely incidental to entertainment that is provided for customers, agents, promoters etc. It must be an annual event and not a one-off.

It is possible to have more than one annual event (see HMRC notice EIM21690). The definition of "employee" is extended to include retired members of staff and the partners of existing and past employees. Although the expenditure is allowable, the employees themselves may have to pay tax on the entertainment received and the employer will have to report this on form P11D. It should be noted that this is an exemption and not an allowance, so if the cost of the event is £40 per employee, you can only exempt out £40 per person and not take an allowance of £150 per person.

Musicians' fees

For musicians who run a band, quartets, orchestras or similar groups, the fees paid to other musicians are an allowable expense. However, you must declare the full income of the gig you have arranged and show the other musicians' costs as expenses. The musicians should invoice the organiser for their agreed fee. The invoicing musicians  should state that they are responsible for their own income tax and National Insurance. It may be considered that the other musicians are employees of the organiser, so check the HMRC Employment Status Indicator at http://bit.ly/ESI–AUG18. If the musician can install a deputy, then this should be enough for them not to be an employee.

Other costs

Health and fitness expenditure

As an actor and performer it's important to keep yourself in good shape and looking good. It may be necessary for an actor to incur specific cosmetic surgery costs solely for the purposes of their career. Your agent may advise you to have your teeth whitened or even straightened as this could be holding back your TV or film career. Such expenses may be deductible, but the tax authorities are quite strict in this area, so talk to your accountant about this. In most cases, any medical treatment is not allowable as an expense as it has dual benefit.

A regular visit to the chiropractor would not be an allowable expense as the outcome of the treatment is not wholly for the business. The cost of osteopathy or physiotherapy cannot be claimed even where the treatment arises specifically from the strains of playing an instrument. If you feel you have incurred private medical costs for something specific that only occurred through your self-employment and you could not wait for NHS treatment, then you could make a claim for the cost, but declare it in the "Other information" section and then HMRC can make a call on it.

Your monthly or annual gym membership cost may be deductible, but it is dependent on what you do. In most cases it will not be an allowable cost as HMRC deem it a dual benefit of improving your health or keeping healthy and there are alternatives. However, if the only option is working in a gym, then it could be allowable e.g. the business is a cage fighter and you need specialist equipment. There is a paragraph on the HMRC website that clearly states that gym membership is not an allowable expense. I know you won't believe me, so here is the link: http://bit.ly/HMRC-GYM.

Subscriptions

You can claim for:

- trade or professional journals
- trade body or professional organisation membership if related to your business

You can not claim for:

- payments to political parties
- gym membership fees
- donations to charity - but you may be able to claim for sponsorship payments

---

So although you think you need to look good for your public and have a buff body, don't even think about expensing your gym membership and general health classes like yoga, Pilates etc.

Insurance

This is normally the cost of insuring yourself and your business, especially public liability insurance and professional indemnity insurance if you are involved in training and article writing that people may rely and act on. Public liability insurance is generally covered by membership to a union, for example Equity or the Musicians' Union.

Other insurances are available, for example, insurance for a pianist's fingers or dancer's legs, and these are all valid costs as wholly and exclusively used for the business of being a performer. For more on insurance, see Chapter 20.

Observation

The number of clients that present to me a list of all their expenditure from their business bank account. Nothing too much wrong with that, assuming it is backed up by receipts. However, it is when they add in payments for their tax bill as an allowable expense that I smile.

Sorry – paying your tax bill is not an allowable expense in the following year, and nor is the payment on account (more of that later) or National Insurance payments.

Things you need to do

☐ Do you know what each receipt is for?

☐ Can you justify each spend as wholly and exclusively for your business?

☐ Have you updated the record keeping for each spend?

☐ Are there items you are unsure of? If so, get professional advice.

CHAPTER 12:

Can I have a receipt or invoice please?

As per the section on bookkeeping (Chapter 8), it is vital that you have back-up for the costs that you plan to claim against your fee income. If there is no supporting documentation, then you run the risk of costs being disallowed.

Where musicians run into difficulty is if they play in quartets, trios, bands etc and one person takes charge as an unofficial partnership. The controller of this should take all the income as their income and the payments to the other musicians are allowable costs. But often the other musicians do not invoice for the gig, so their income records are incomplete and the controller has no record of the costs. The answer obviously is for the musicians to invoice, but if that is not possible, then the controller can use a duplicate receipt book and get the musicians to sign for their money, so the receipt book acts as income and expenditure for the different parties.

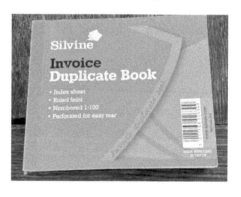

"I have a receipt here. It has no value on it. Does that matter?"

This is a question I have been asked a few times but, yes, you do have to have a receipt with a value on it, otherwise we have no idea what to claim. A delivery note is just that. It shows what was delivered (or packed) and not how much it was. That'll be on an invoice. An order confirmation? That's just an order. It might have a value on it but it's not an invoice.

The typical supplier here is Amazon. You can place an order, you'll get an order confirmation, but you need to go onto your Amazon account and download the receipt. Often there is a button there that says, "Print invoice", "Invoice 1", "Request invoice". That's what you need to collect.

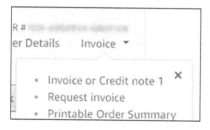
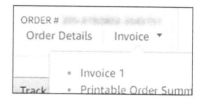

Beware of the one that says, "Invoice or credit note 1", because that just gives you a delivery document and not an invoice. As you can see, it gives no value, and is just a packing slip. If you get this, you need to request the invoice.

Sometimes you get lucky and there is the option to print the invoice. That is what you need.

If you go the Post Office and say you want something recorded, they'll give you a little slip that says, "Here's your proof of posting and this is the tracking number". It doesn't have a value on it, so you still need to get the receipt from the Post Office.

Another of the main examples here is subsistence and entertaining. It is such an old chestnut. The receipt should tell you what you have purchased. What have you eaten? What have you drunk? And with any luck, it'll have the number of people that were round the table, so the number of guests. If it's just for you, I would expect that the amount to be, let's be generous, say £15 or less. Any more than that and it would then question if it was just you eating or if there was someone else there and in effect you were entertaining somebody? Entertainment is not an allowable expense for the self-employed.

It's actually not an allowable expense for a company but it goes through as company business and then gets disregarded for the tax return.

I know it sounds like a painful thing to do but always, always, always ask for a VAT receipt, whether you are registered for VAT or not. It'll just state exactly what you have purchased, and then it can be established if it is relevant for your business. It is a key document for your tax return. Any problems, ask a qualified accountant, and they should be able to give you plenty of examples of what to look for and not to look for, and how to get that invoice.

Some people use apps to record costs by taking a photo of them and it then goes through an optical character recognition process and the data can be downloaded when needed. But the data you get out is only as good as the data you put in. You need to ensure that the following is in focus and visible on the picture:

- ♫ Supplier name
- ♫ Date
- ♫ Amount
- ♫ Description

Without this, the costs may not be captured correctly if at all. Beware of the double-sided receipts (such as Sainsbury's) as the data is on the reverse. Not very helpful, but it does cut down on paper. You may want to write on the receipt before you take the picture to remind yourself what the spend was for, and then it can be tagged in the app, or analysed on the spreadsheet correctly.

What about debit and credit card receipts?

People ask about credit card receipts and debit card receipts. Well, they are not really an allowable receipt for your business. The reason being there's no detail on what was purchased, there's no evidence that the purchases are wholly and exclusively for your business and if you're registered for VAT there's no split on the VAT account. So really, using debit or credit card receipts does not give you the effective accounting and bookkeeping records that you need. What you always need to do is make sure that when you go into a store, you get a proper till receipt or a proper itemised receipt that you can use for your business.

If you're using an online accounting system or an app, then you need to make sure you only take the picture of the full receipt and not the debit card because the system's going to think they're two different receipts and it's going to book it twice. Me, as an accountant, when I get a shoebox of stuff, the first thing I do is put everything into date order and match the credit card receipts and the debit card receipt to the actual receipt. It takes a lot of time, so if you're paying an hourly rate, you may want to do it yourself.

Once you have matched the credit card receipt to the actual receipt, only put through the actual receipt for your bookkeeping, and then if you do spend cash, separate it out. Always collect the proper receipt, especially if it's something for entertaining or subsistence. If I see a receipt for McDonald's say, for £30, I know it's not just for you, unless you're very, very hungry. So a debit card receipt for that goes straight to entertaining. Ignore the debit card and credit card receipts, go for a proper receipt, and use those in your bookkeeping. Thank you.

Non-GBP receipts

What happens if you get a receipt in a foreign currency? Well, it's actually quite easy to deal with. Receipts should be translated on the date of the spend, or potentially if you're using cash, the exchange rate you used when you got the currency in the first place. If you use a UK debit card or credit card then it'll be the rate that the bank did the conversion at.

Now the only things you should be claiming as part of your business are things that are wholly and exclusively for your self-employment. That sightseeing trip around Athens and the Parthenon, that really is not an allowable expense just because you happened to be in Greece on a concert tour. My advice to you would be to write on the top of the receipt what it was for, because your accountant may not be able to read Greek. My language ability is not brilliant, and 18 months later, are you going to be able to remember what that receipt was for?

If you are using scanning software to get your information into your accounts, then do not scan the foreign currency receipts unless you have an accounting system that deals with multiple currency. Most don't. So hold on to those and you or your accountants can add them in at the end. However, some apps link to exchange rates and will translate automatically, but it may not be the rate that appears on your bank statement or credit card bill. You can change the GBP value in these apps, although you may not be too bothered as the difference will probably be minuscule. Some people go off into Europe plenty of times and may have a Euro account. What you then do for any of the transactions that go through the Euro account is just use an average of exchange rate for the month, and then put that in your books. You can find the average exchange rate. Just Google "HMRC monthly exchange rates" for, let's say, 2018, and a website will pop up where those exchange rates are. The current year, the current month, will be at the very top.

If you do spend a lot of time abroad, it will be worthwhile having a foreign currency account. It'll save an awful lot of exchange charges because as you know banks will charge for anything, so every time you do a purchase in the foreign currency it will charge you a transaction fee.

Things you need to do

- ☐ Ensure that all bits of paper have values on them.

- ☐ Check you have an appropriate exchange rate, either from the bank or HMRC website.

- ☐ Ensure you have full receipts, not just the credit or debit card receipt.

- ☐ Have you accounted for all cash spend? Remember those pesky car parking charges.

- ☐ Make sure people sign for payments if they don't give you a receipt, for example deputies or teachers.

CHAPTER 13:

Do I need an accounting system? What should I use?

A question frequently asked by people going into the arts, entertainment and music industry as a performer is whether they should keep their accounting records on some kind of system. The answer is, it depends. What do you mean, a system? A system could be that you get receipts and you put them in an envelope by month, or you throw them in a shoebox in the corner, or you might keep them in your wallet or your handbag. It's a system, but it doesn't necessarily work. Or do you mean do you need to have an accounting system to set up and record all your invoices and costs, etc?

Clearly they are two extremes, but yes, you should have some sort of system in place. As an accountant, I always advocate processes and systems, but there are different types. You can have a manual cash book which is a physical book to record your incomings and your outgoings. That is a system. Providing you add it up at the end of each month or at the end of each page, then that will work. You don't get much analysis out of it unless you buy one of those really big long red books and you split it into different types of spend and different types of income.

You could set up an Excel spreadsheet. Yes, other spreadsheet systems are available, but I'm an old-fashioned person and Excel works fine for me. You can set up a whole series of sheets in a workbook recording your income, costs, mileage and other allowance calculations. You can do all sorts of analysis on it. Providing it gets you to the end result you need, that's great. Make sure you remember everything that is business related – allowable costs as discussed in Chapter 11.

You could go a stage further if you're not happy using spreadsheets and use one of these apps I have mentioned previously where you are able to take a photo of your receipt or your invoice coming in and it will wing off into the internet, and you'll get back effectively some kind of file, either every month, every quarter or every year that you can download. Hopefully, if you've coded everything correctly as you send it in (for example for your train ticket you've actually put it against travel and not against a utility bill), then at least what you get back should make some sense as to what you've done in the year.

Finally, you get accounting systems that you can use on their own or with another receipt scanning app. You can manually key into the accounting system what you spend (or use an app), and your income. The accounting system can produce your own invoices for you. You can even have things that link it to your business bank account. Now when I say business bank account I don't mean a proper business bank account. It could just be a personal account you earmark for your self-employed business. You can link all that through. It will take a lot of the grunt work out of bookkeeping. With all the technology available now, it does make life easier for the self-employed, but just be on the ball.

Obviously I've gone from something that's very cheap to costing virtually nothing to use like pieces of paper and pen, through to an all-encompassing accounting system for small businesses. They range in price and they range in complexity. Sometimes it might be a case of  you are cash-rich and time-poor, so therefore a scanning solution might be the operation for you. Or you're very cash-poor but time-rich so you might want to do your own Excel spreadsheets. Obviously there is the answer that you could get an accountant or a bookkeeper to do it for you, but I don't want to flog our services too much.

I personally prefer the accounting system and an application to take photos of my receipts, but if all else fails, just get an app to take photos of your receipts and receiving invoices and get the app to do that main bookkeeping work for you. So much easier than sitting there for days on end trying to make sense of what's going into the bank statement, what haven't I got, where are my receipts, which handbag did I use, etc. You might as well set something up at the beginning. When you've been to a shop, and you've bought what you needed, write on the top of it what it was for, take a photo of it, and then when you get home by all means throw the receipt into a shoebox and then label the shoebox for the year.

Now the government has decided it wants to have small businesses, actually any business, record their costs and their income electronically, and you have to have digital records. If your turnover is over the VAT threshold (see http://performanceaccountancy.co.uk/rates/ for the current threshold) then quarterly electronic reporting for VAT is coming in from April 2019. It might be a spreadsheet and some kind of widget that takes the figures off the spreadsheet and sends it to HMRC. It might be a phone app that does the same thing, or it could be an accounting system. But it will be quarterly (unless you are doing monthly VAT returns) and it will be mandated for those whose turnover is over the VAT threshold.

You may think you have escaped, but be aware that any sole trader/self-employed person, or even a landlord that earns over £10,000 of income before allowable costs, will have to start keeping their records electronically, and finding a method to report these numbers to HMRC. The agent portal to your tax return will disappear and we will have to buy specialist software to be able to do that (note to self, fee will have to go up). At the moment it's billed to be no earlier than April 2020. With all the problems at HMRC and the other big projects they have going on, it may come into force in stages.

Why not start now from the beginning of the next tax year, get used to it, and build it up. You've then got your records going back and making your life easier. If you're worried about the cost, then just get a single scanning app. I'm sure you can get them quite cheaply down to nothing, or we do licence one that people can use which has a monthly fee. I'm not pushing my services, but if you do need help and advice on setting up a system, then book a call in with me at https://performanceaccountancy.youcanbook.me/.

Consider the system use, and then also look at the use of an accountant or a bookkeeper. They can make life so much easier for you, but you do have to be organised and you have to have some kind of process in place. When you've finished collecting a month or quarter year of receipts, you could send them to the bookkeeper or accountant, to work on. Get some kind of process sorted so it's not a panic on, let's say, 29 January, when you're trying to do your tax return.

Things you need to do

- ☐ Decide how you are going to do your record keeping.

- ☐ If using an app, make sure you have access to it via your phone, tablet and computer (yes, I do mean a Mac as well as a PC).

- ☐ Invite in your accountant if you have one. Consider buying a licence from your accountant and wrap up some support into the deal.

- ☐ Think about storing the physical receipts if you are using an upload system for a couple of years "just in case", and then ensure you have access to the online version before throwing them away.

- ☐ Give the app a chance and remember to use it.

CHAPTER 14:
Income and costs from overseas engagements

As a self-employed performer, you are likely to be asked to go overseas for performances, either as a singer or musician for a concert or production, an actor for filming, or even just to audition overseas.

If you work abroad, it is possible that you will be taxed on the income in that country and then potentially face being taxed on the same income in the UK as the UK tax system is based on worldwide income. Effectively you get taxed twice – not good news. See Chapter 6 regarding sorting out your A1/E101 form before you start to work abroad.

The good news is that when you prepare your UK tax return, you can often claim relief for some or all of the tax paid overseas which is part of the double tax treaty that the UK has with various other countries. There is a list on the HMRC website showing which countries there are already double tax treaties with, and those in progress.

In general, your combined tax bill on overseas income should not be more than the amount of UK tax on that income.

For example, if you earned £16,000 in a year from overseas which was taxed at 15%, then you would have received £13,600. Some people would declare the £13,600 and pay tax at 20% in the UK so paying out another £2,720. What you should actually do on the UK self-assessment tax return is declare £16,000, suffer a 20% deduction of £3,200 and claim the tax already paid of £2,720. Therefore £800 would be the amount payable in the UK.

If you happen to have paid more than 20% tax overseas, the UK government **does not** give a rebate and that extra tax paid to the overseas country is lost!

And here is the BUT. Well two actually.

BUT 1 – In order to claim the double tax credit, you must have a certificate of tax deducted from the overseas country.

BUT 2 – The UK tax credit allowed by HMRC is normally calculated on your net profit for your overseas earnings. So you have your income from abroad, less your costs, gives you your profit. 20% tax is then applied. If on the above example your costs were £7,000, you would be taxed at 20% on £9,000 so giving you a potential tax bill of £1,800. You've already paid £2,720 so no more to pay. Sadly there's no refund either.

Actually there is a third BUT. The treaty between the UK and another country may restrict the amount of tax that can be taken as a foreign tax credit, and that in turn is dependent on the type of income. You may have suffered 20% deduction from a Spanish dividend, but the maximum credit given is only 15%, therefore the full amount cannot be offset against UK tax.

Bear in mind, for overseas earnings for self-employment, you will probably be deducted the in-country tax as withholding tax, plus their own form of social security which is not recoverable against the UK tax system. That is why you should get your A1 certificate sorted before you travel. This was covered in Chapter 6.

I've known people to put the full amount of overseas tax credit as an expense within the business accounts rather than claim the credit under the double taxation treaty. This is not correct – don't even think about it.

Overseas expenses

Given you get income from your performances abroad, you are bound to have expenses such as living accommodation, food, drink and travel. These expenses are allowable against the income. However, personal expenses are not an allowable tax deduction, and always be aware of issues if you take family members or non-business associates away with you as their costs will not be allowable (I touched on this earlier).

Completing the self-assessment form using foreign tax credit relief

When completing the self-assessment tax return, foreign income should be put as part of your business income and not in the "Foreign" section of the tax return. However, if you want to claim foreign tax credit relief on this income you should complete the "Foreign tax paid on employment, self-employment and partnership" sections of the foreign pages. It is so much easier to complete this section online, rather than on a paper return.

Fill in your return
Foreign income details (Page 2 of 2)

If you are claiming foreign tax credit relief for any of your foreign income, there will be a few extra steps to complete immediately prior to viewing your full tax calculation.

You said that you received foreign income in the tax year 6 April 2017 to 5 April 2018. Please complete the following question(s).

Which of the following **types of income or gain** did you receive from overseas sources?

☐ Interest and other income from overseas savings (Optional) ❓

☐ Dividends from foreign companies (Optional) ❓

☐ Overseas pensions, social security benefits and royalties etc (Optional) ❓

☐ Dividend income received by a person abroad (Optional) ❓

☐ All other income received by a person abroad **and** any remitted 'ring fenced' foreign income (Optional) ❓

☐ Employment, self-employment and other income which you paid foreign tax on (Optional) ❓

☐ Capital gains (Optional) ❓

☐ Any other overseas income and gains (Optional) ❓

☐ Income from land and property abroad (Optional) ❓

✖ Delete foreign section

Save and continue

The bits of information you need are:

- ♫ A reference to know which piece of work you are referring to – it is only your reference

- ♫ The country where the work was performed

- ♫ The amount of income tax/withholding tax deducted in GBP

- ♫ Gross amount earned in GBP before any deductions.

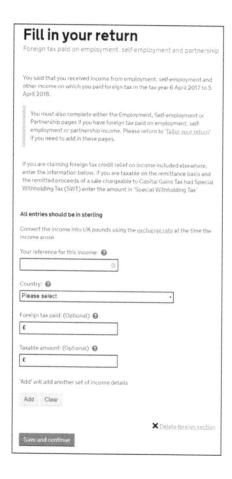

The final bit to do would be to claim the foreign tax relief which comes right at the end of the tax return. That page can look daunting, so seek help if you are not sure.

Things you need to do

☐ Obtain copies of withholding tax certificates.

☐ Make sure you have remittance advices.

☐ Know the amount of gross earnings and split of deductions.

☐ Currency transfer fees are allowable costs, so don't forget to include them in the expenses file.

CHAPTER 15:

Capital allowances

Capital allowances... Ah yes, the bit on the tax return that makes people go "urgggg – what is this". Well, I am going to try and make it simple for you. You may think capital is that big combine harvester in the field, or the silos that store Angel Delight mix (do they still make that in Banbury?), but a piece of capital equipment can be anything that lasts normally over two years and has a significant value to you and your business. Some things may pass the length of time test, but don't cost very much, for example an inkjet printer can last a few years (it may be out of date a week after you buy it), but for £50 it's not that much in value.

Typical capital items that are used for a business and professional use are:

- ♫ Computer
- ♫ Mobile phone
- ♫ Car (special rules so beware)
- ♫ Office equipment
- ♫ Furniture
- ♫ Musical instruments

It is really useful to keep records of these types of purchases separate from your normal accounting records as they must be kept and dealt with separately. Whilst the asset is still in use and has value, you need to have access to those records.

These types of purchases can all attract capital allowances for the business. However, if there is some element of personal use, only the business proportion of the item's cost can be treated as an allowance for the business.

If you keep business accounts, then you would do something called depreciation, which recognises the cost of these items over their useful lives. Normally it is three or five years as that is the length of time that the business will get benefit from the items.

However, the tax man likes to be different. He will not allow a business to decide what depreciation rate they will apply to their business, so will disallow any costs charged to the accounts for depreciation. They will allow a "writing down allowance" which gives a tax allowance for purchasing capital for the business over time. The main differences are the rate it allows and the method applied.

What do I mean by that? Well, a business would buy a computer that lasts three years, so split the cost over three years and allocate an equal amount each year and then the asset has a value of zero at the end of the three years even if still in use. The tax man allows an 18% writing down allowance per year, but it is based on the net residual value at the time. This means that the asset will never be fully written off whilst it is still in use in the business.

If we take the example of buying an Apple Mac and saying it will last for three years, this is what we would get:

	Accounts	Tax
Purchased 20 June 2018	1,500.00	1,500.00
Depreciation @ 33%	500.00	
WDA[1] @ 18%		270.00
Value 31 March 2019	1,000.00	1,230.00
Depreciation @ 33%	500.00	
WDA @ 18%		221.40
Value 31 March 2020	500.00	1,008.60
Depreciation @ 33%	500.00	181.55
WDA @ 18%		
Value 31 March 2021	0.00	827.05
Depreciation @ 33%	–	148.87
WDA @ 18%		
Value 31 March 2022	0.00	678.18
Depreciation @ 33%	–	122.07
WDA @ 18%		
Value 31 March 2023	0.00	556.11

All assets are treated like this (except cars and private use assets), and they go into a general pool of assets. If the value of the general pool goes below £1,000, then the business can claim a writing down allowance (WDA) of the final balance of the pool.

"But that's not fair," I hear you say. When is taxation fair? When you get rid of the asset and according to your tax accounts it still has a value, you can take the final tax value of the asset as an allowance in the year the asset was disposed of. If you sold it for more than it is worth on your tax books, you have to pay money back to the tax man. If that happens, please contact your accountant on how to treat it.

1. WDA is the writing down allowance, normally at 18%, but some cars are at 8%.

There is a bit of good news that helps the small business. If you spend money on capital items, then you may qualify to count them as part of the annual investment allowance. This is an allowance the government gives businesses as a tax allowance so that if they spend up to £25k in a year (this amount can change each year), it can all be written against this allowance in the year of purchase. If you don't spend £25k, you don't get the difference paid to you!

Of course, if you sold an asset that you'd written off as part of this annual investment allowance, then you will have to make an adjustment in the year of sale.

Capital allowances and cars

Oh, what fun.

The capital allowance on cars is based on the CO_2 emission of a car and when the car was purchased. The younger the car and the lower the emissions, then the better off you are with capital allowances. It even gets to the stage that the really low emission cars can be written off in the year they were purchased. The capital allowance for a low emission car is 18%, but other cars are 8%. You can only claim a capital allowance on the car if you are using the actual cost method of car costs and not the mileage basis. As with other items of capital, the allowance needs to be reduced if there is any personal use of the car.

I would always seek advice in this area. Sometimes the definition of a car and van are not very clear.

On the good news side, if you are a driving instructor and your car is fitted with dual controls, it is not deemed to be a car with personal use as the dual control gets in the way of personal benefit. Dual control cars are treated as plant and machinery and therefore the normal capital allowance (WDA) applies and you can use it against the annual investment allowance. For my clients, we have treated it as a standard pool asset in case there is a sale and a profit is made. I do like to be cautious at times.

Story:

I was at a conference giving a lecture on the joys of financial admin. At the end of the session, one of the attendees came up to me and questioned what I said about capital allowances and the use of a car.

It turned out she was claiming the mileage allowance as well as DVLA costs, insurance and servicing. Worse than that, she put the whole cost of the car down as a capital allowance instead of the 8% capital allowance, and with no restriction for personal use.

Luckily the tax return had not been submitted to HMRC, so we were able to show what needed to be put into the capital allowance box and how the personal use restriction worked, but it meant she had a tax bill to pay rather than nothing.

Result – a happy client because it did not raise any issues with HMRC, and an unhappy client as she had to find the money to pay her tax bill after buying a car. Can't win 'em all I guess.

Overview

Here is a flowchart to make the understanding of capital allowances easier.

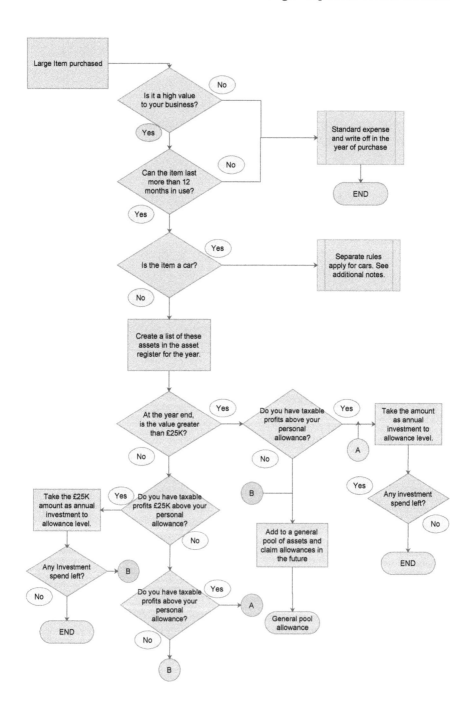

Things you need to do

- ☐ Keep your receipts carefully for capital items as the cost can be expensed over several years.

- ☐ Keep detailed accounting logs of these items and capital allowance charged each year – per item.

- ☐ Remember if you sell or dispose, you may have an extra tax to pay, or can claim more of an allowance.

- ☐ If the asset has some personal use, then you can only claim a percentage of the capital allowance for the year.

SECTION 4:

What else do I need to know?

CHAPTER 16:

Student loans

If you have a student loan, it will have to be repaid depending on the plan type and depending on your income level. If you have a PAYE job, and your weekly or monthly pay looks like you will be over the repayment threshold, the employer will deduct an amount each week or month. However, for self-employed musicians and actors, we won't know how much to repay until the self-assessment tax return is filed.

Full-time students only need to start to repay at the earliest in the April in the year after they graduated (or left if the course was not completed). This is irrespective of how long the course is. If you have a student loan plan one, and your self-employed and other employment income and profit is greater than £18,330 (2018/2019) you will then need to start repaying your student loan at 9% for that year. If you are on plan two, then your PAYE income and your self-employed profit needs to total more than £25,000 and then you start to repay at 9%. These rates change each year.

The fun starts if you have two different loan plans, as you could be paying back on one loan and not the other. If you are earning over the plan two threshold, the amounts being paid back go towards both loans.

With PAYE if you leave a job in the middle of the year, your P45 does not show your student loan payments. So, when it comes to doing your tax return you may have to get a statement from the Student Loans Company for the whole tax year to look at how much has actually been paid in. Your P60 for any employer at the end of the year will only show student loan taken for that employment. It does not take into account any employment prior in that tax year.

It is possible to get a refund of student loan if:

- ♪ Repayments were taken but total earnings were less than the threshold.
- ♪ If everything has been repaid, but deductions have still been taken.

Overpayments often happen with a PAYE job, but then a loss is made in the self-employment. The refund has to be obtained from the Student Loans Company and evidence of overpayment sent, normally P60 and/or payslips.

Of course, there may be a bit of a concern about whether the debt will ever be repaid. You stop owing money once the debt has been repaid, or when the debt is 30 years old from the April after you graduated. You could always become a mature student at 50, and potentially you may never have to repay the loan.

When it comes to the self-assessment bill, you need to ensure you not only factor in 20% (or 40%) income tax and 9% National Insurance but also the 9% student loan repayment, and more than likely a 50% payment on account. That's a lot of money to find on 31 January. As an example, a plan one student earning £35,000 with £12,560 of costs has tax to pay of £5,233 which is 23.32% of taxable income.

Assume 2018/2019 figures	
Fee income	35,000
Expenses	12,560
Taxable income	22,440
Personal allowance	11,850
Income tax	2,118.00
Class 4 NI	1,284.84
Student loan plan 1	129.60
Payment on account	1,701.42
Payment on 31 Jan	5,233.86
Payment on 31 July	1,701.42

What do we learn from this?

If you have a student loan, put aside at least 20% of all your fee income (before costs) into a savings account to make sure you have enough set aside to pay the bill when needed.

Student loans for the self employed

Complete the loan question in the tax return on paper or online

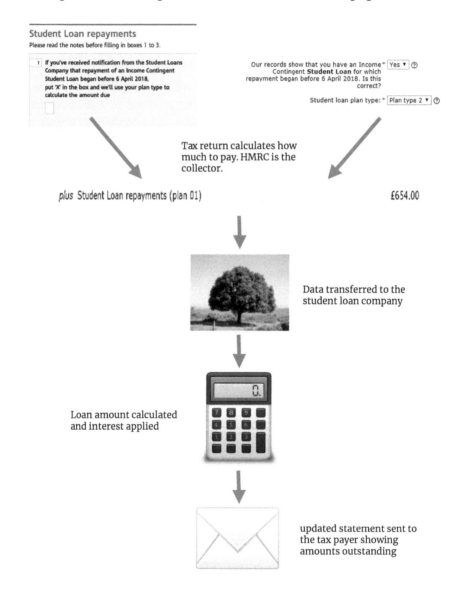

Student Loan repayments
Please read the notes before filling in boxes 1 to 3.

1 **If you've received notification from the Student Loans Company that repayment of an Income Contingent Student Loan began before 6 April 2018,** put 'X' in the box and we'll use your plan type to calculate the amount due

Our records show that you have an Income Contingent **Student Loan** for which repayment began before 6 April 2018. Is this correct?   Yes ▾ ⑦

Student loan plan type: * Plan type 2 ▾ ⑦

Tax return calculates how much to pay. HMRC is the collector.

plus Student Loan repayments (plan 01)   £654.00

Data transferred to the student loan company

Loan amount calculated and interest applied

updated statement sent to the tax payer showing amounts outstanding

Things you need to do

☐   If you have a student loan, know which plan you are on.

☐   Keep a record of how much your employer has taken from you each month. It is NOT on the P45.

☐   Keep your statements from the Student Loans Company especially when getting near to the completion of the loan amount.

CHAPTER 17:
Penalties for late tax returns

In this chapter, I'm looking at what happens if you submit your tax return late.

Should you receive a letter from HMRC stating you have to complete a tax return, you are legally obliged to complete it, even if you think it is not relevant to you. If you consider that you do not need to submit a tax return, for example because all your income is taxed under PAYE, you can phone HMRC and ask for the tax return to be withdrawn. If HMRC agrees and withdraws the return, it means that you do not have to file a return and any penalties issued for missing the tax return filing deadline will be set aside.

Completing and filing a tax return

Assuming that you are going to have to complete the return, you need to stick to very strict deadlines. Can I remind you that if you are going to file on paper, the return must reach HMRC by 31 October following the end of that tax year. There have been all sorts of stories about people driving to their local HMRC on deadline day just to make sure they got the paperwork in just before midnight and the day ticking over to 1 November.

Of course, there is still the 31 January following the end of the tax year to do an online filing. It gives you more time to procrastinate and wallow about it over the holiday season.

Online filing has increased over the years. 2005/2006 saw 23% of returns filed online, compared to 93.47% for 2016/2017. Statistics issued by HMRC for the tax year 2016/2017 showed that 6,033 people avoided wrapping Christmas gifts and filed their return on Christmas Eve, 2,590 on Christmas Day and a further 7,655 on Boxing Day. Anything to get out of the cooking, cleaning up, or the in-laws I guess. More worrying though is that 758,707 filed their returns on 31 January 2018 with several thousand people filing in the last few hours. What if your internet connection failed? That is scary. 6.5% of people that were due to complete a return did not file on time.

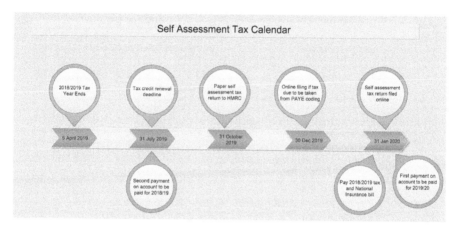

Penalties for late tax return submission

As I mentioned earlier, there are penalties for late submission of your return (in addition to late payment of tax), and these can mount up considerably. These charges are applied even if you have no tax to pay.

A tax return submitted after 31 January will have an initial £100 penalty applied. The bad thing about the online system is that HMRC know if you are even just five minutes late, so make sure your clock is accurate if you're leaving it this late!

If you don't submit for more than three months, there are penalties of £10 per day for a period of three months. This means you can pay an ADDITIONAL £900 in penalties.

From six months late, there is an additional £300 or 5% of the tax owed – whichever is the greater.

Over 12 months late, a further £300 or 5% of tax is due, whichever is greater, but with more serious cases, it could be 100% of the tax due.

Period	HMRC - Self Assessment
1 day to 1 month	
1 day to 3 months	£100
1 to 3 months	
3 to 6 months	Add £10 per day
6 to 12 months	Add 5% of tax due or £300 if greater
Over 12 months	Add 5% of tax due or £300 if greater

Paper returns have similar penalties in place, but the start point is 31 October!

There are also penalties for late payment of tax if you didn't think the above was bad enough.

Late Payment	Penalty
30 days late	5% of tax due
6 months late	5% of tax outstanding at that date
12 months late	5% of tax outstanding at that date

Reasonable excuses for a late tax return

HMRC does allow a reasonable excuse for a late tax return. A reasonable excuse is when some unforeseen or unusual event beyond your control has prevented you from filing the return on time.

Examples of "reasonable excuse" from the HMRC website are:

♪ A failure in the HMRC computer system.

♪ Your computer breaks down just before or during the preparation of your online return.

♫ A serious illness, disability or serious mental health condition has made you incapable of filing your tax return.

♫ You registered for HMRC Online Services but didn't get your Activation code in time.

Each case is unique and will be assessed in its own right.

One excuse I hear time and time again is that people do their return and save it, but never press the submit button.

A direct extract from the HMRC/GOV website gives these as the top 10 oddest excuses for not filing a tax return on time. I can relate to the last one. I suggest you don't use these!

♫ My pet goldfish died (self-employed builder).

♫ I had a run-in with a cow (Midlands farmer).

♫ After seeing a volcanic eruption on the news, I couldn't concentrate on anything else (London woman).

♫ My wife won't give me my mail (self-employed trader).

♫ My husband told me the deadline was 31 March, and I believed him (Leicester hairdresser).

♫ I've been far too busy touring the country with my one-man play (Coventry writer).

♫ My bad back means I can't go upstairs. That's where my tax return is (a working taxi driver).

♫ I've been cruising round the world in my yacht, and only picking up post when I'm on dry land (South East man).

♫ Our business doesn't really do anything (Kent financial services firm).

♫ I've been too busy submitting my clients' tax returns (London accountant).

HMRC did issue an updated list of excuses, and they made me smile.

- ♪ I couldn't file my return on time as my wife has been seeing aliens and won't let me enter the house.

- ♪ My ex-wife left my tax return upstairs, but I suffer from vertigo and can't go to retrieve it.

- ♪ I spilt coffee on it.

So get cracking. The HMRC helpline number if you have been issued a tax return and you don't think you should have one, is 0300 200 3310 and it is open Monday to Friday 8am to 8pm and Saturday 8am to 4pm, and they are even open on Sundays.

Things you need to do

- ☐ Do your tax return early so there's no stress, as things can happen.

- ☐ Don't file late – the £100 fine can buy a lovely pair of shoes.

- ☐ Don't pay late – the 5% interest can buy shoe polish.

CHAPTER 18:

Gift Aid and contributions to charity

A quick note about Gift Aid and gifting to charities. As you may know, if you gift money to charities, then potentially a charity can reclaim something called Gift Aid. They get to claim 25% back from HMRC. This does assume that you are a UK resident and a taxpayer paying tax. What many people don't appreciate is the benefit of Gift Aid, especially the higher rate taxpayers. Whilst the benefit of giving to charity for the basic rate taxpayers might not be as pronounced as the higher rate or additional rate, those on the cusp of the 20 to 40% threshold should really take note. For higher or additional rate taxpayers, by gifting money to charity you are essentially widening your basic rate band and therefore more of your income is taxed at the lower band, which reduces the tax at higher rate.

As an example, if somebody earning say £50,000 gifts £2,000 to charity, they would see their basic rate threshold climb from the £45,000 to £47,000. Rather than pay 40% tax on earnings over £45,000, they would only pay this rate on earnings above £47,000. That saves £400 in tax. This is based on the 2017/2018 tax returns. As charity gains 25% Gift Aid, the charity would actually receive a £2,500 donation, which would cost a higher rate taxpayer £1,600 net.

Simple cash donations to people on the street or donating coins into a charity box don't actually attract the same benefits. You have to have signed a Gift Aid form. A lot of people do sign Gift Aid forms, but don't keep a copy of the form. Therefore, you can't easily prove that you have made these Gift Aid payments.

If you are wealthy, there are no limits on the amount that can be given to charity and potentially you could backdate claims of charitable giving.

Now, there is a bum side to it. If you do Gift Aid and you declare you are a taxpayer, but actually it works out that you're below the personal allowance, then in effect, you will have to pay over the 25% Gift Aid that the charity will receive. They can't claim back tax on tax that's never been paid, so that's why you might see in your tax return a charity tax and that's because you have given money to charity, ticked the Gift Aid box, but you haven't made any tax contributions to allow that to happen. Just be careful when you sign those Gift Aid forms that you realise what you're actually signing up to, and if you don't think your income's going to be high enough to pay tax, don't tick the Gift Aid box.

Things you need to do

- ☐ Keep a copy of any Gift Aid form you sign.

- ☐ Keep records of any online transactions like Just Giving.

- ☐ If you are not a taxpayer, don't sign with Gift Aid.

CHAPTER 19:

VAT – an overview

OK – this is another really dry topic. I'm so sorry. However, if your fee income from self-employment is nowhere near the current threshold (https://performanceaccountancy.co.uk/rates/) then don't worry about this section.

What is VAT?

Value Added Tax (VAT) is an amount charged on most goods and services that are purchased in the UK and equivalent in Europe. A business registered for VAT will charge it on to other business and consumers in the UK. The good thing is that VAT registered businesses are able to reclaim the amount of VAT that has been charged to them. The bad thing is that non-VAT registered businesses and consumers are not able to claim back the VAT. Effectively it is a sale of goods tax to consumers.

Currently in the UK, there are three rates of VAT and an exemption rate:

- ♫ Standard rate VAT – is the one we know at 20%
- ♫ Reduced rate VAT – mainly utilities at 5%
- ♫ Zero rate VAT – being 0%
- ♫ Exempt VAT – has no rate and does not carry any VAT charge and those that are outside the UK VAT system altogether.

This brief chapter takes you through standard VAT. A further guide will be available in the future looking at some of the areas in detail, but still hopefully in a simplistic easy to understand way.

VAT is not just for companies, but it applies to anyone in business whether they are a sole trader, partnership, charity or company. The list of "legal entities" that have to be VAT registered if they are in business are:

- ♫ An individual
- ♫ A partnership
- ♫ A company
- ♫ A club
- ♫ An association
- ♫ A charity
- ♫ Any other organisation or group of people acting together under a particular name, such as an educational or health institution, exhibition, conference, etc
- ♫ A trust
- ♫ A local authority

VAT is reported (and paid for) on a quarterly basis. The months go:

- ♫ Jan/Feb/Mar, Apr/May/June, July/Aug/Sept, Oct/Nov/Dec
- ♫ Feb/Mar/Apr, May/June/July, Aug/Sept/Oct, Nov/Dec/Jan
- ♫ Mar/Apr/May, June/July/Aug, Sept/Oct/Nov, Dec/Jan/Feb

It is possible to ask HMRC for a change in the periods and the most common reason is to align with the business year end.

This infographic will help you to decide whether you should be registered for VAT.

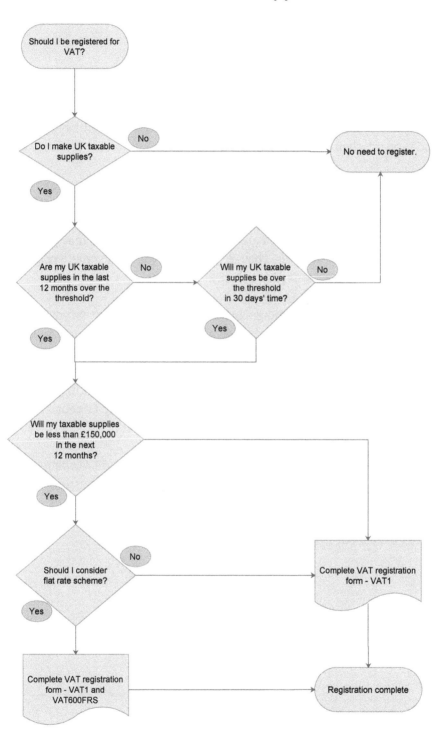

When must I register for VAT?

The UK threshold is set at £85,000 for 2018/2019. However, it is based on a 12-month rolling period so not just for the fiscal year 6 April 2018 to 5 April 2019. If it is likely that your sales of goods and/or services that would be applicable to UK VAT exceeds £85,000 in a 12-month period looking back and forward, then you must register for UK VAT.

A business can register voluntarily for VAT which may give rise to a cash flow benefit, as well as giving perceived comfort to your customers from a marketing perspective, but not being VAT registered may give the impression to prospective clients that you are a small business and this may put them off from using your services. They may feel that you are inexperienced and not able to fulfil their order due to lack of resources.

Of course, there are disadvantages of being VAT registered in that you have to prepare VAT returns on a quarterly basis or employ a bookkeeper or accountant to do it for you. This adds to the cost of doing business. Being VAT registered may make you more expensive to your non-VAT registered customers and less competitive. It would be a case of looking at where most of your income came from and then assessing if you want to register voluntarily. Of course, if you are over the threshold, you have to legally register.

The table below shows a business starting up in January 2018, keeping an eye on its turnover and then seeing that it needed to have been registered for UK VAT in April 2019. This could be based on a sales forecast and if it's proved to be fairly accurate, you would know that the business should start to apply earlier to be ready to charge VAT.

	Invoiced	Dec-18	Jan-19	Feb-19	Mar-19	Apr-19	May-19
Jan-18	400	400					
Feb-18	900	1300	900				
Mar-18	3200	4500	4100	3200			
Apr-18	3780	8280	7880	6980	3780		
May-18	5400	13680	13280	12380	9180	5400	
Jun-18	6500	20180	19780	18880	15680	11900	6500
Jul-18	5620	25800	25400	24500	21300	17520	12120
Aug-18	1200	27000	26600	25700	22500	18720	13320
Sep-18	13500	40500	40100	39200	36000	32220	26820
Oct-18	6950	47450	47050	46150	42950	39170	33770
Nov-18	9752	57202	56802	55902	52702	48922	43522
Dec-18	8900	66102	65702	64802	61602	57822	52422
Jan-19	9970		75672	74772	71572	67792	62392
Feb-19	3457			78229	75029	71249	65849
Mar-19	8660				83689	79909	74509
Apr-19	5500					85409	80009
May-19	14000						94009

Remember that your VAT taxable turnover includes only the goods and services you sell that you have to charge VAT on, even those that are zero-rated. It doesn't include sales that are exempt or outside the scope of VAT.

Are you still with me, 'cos this is carrying on?

What about pre-registration costs?

This is interesting. You can claim back VAT on any items of equipment or stock that was purchased for the business up to four years prior to the registration, provided that the items are still in existence and part of the balance sheet. For services, you can go back six months.

How do I report VAT?

The only way to file a VAT return is online via accounting software or via the HMRC portal. This gives you another seven days to file a return over and above the normal filing deadline on the last day of the month, so now the filing has to be done by the 7th of the second month following the end of the VAT period. Payment needs to be made at the same time that the return is filed. If a direct debit has been set up, HMRC will take the payment several days after the 7th of the month. If a repayment is due, you should file online early as HMRC will do the refund in a few days.

VAT deregistration

It is a fairly simple procedure to deregister for VAT if your turnover has reduced to less than £83,000 (yes, it is a different threshold). If it is going to waver around the threshold, then it is best to stay registered, but if it has reduced significantly, then write to HMRC asking for deregistration. You will need to explain why turnover has dropped so much, for example lost contracts, working hours changed etc, and a 12-month turnover forecast will need to be given.

What are flat rate schemes?

Using the standard rate scheme, you need to record the VAT on every purchase and every sale that is made in the business. However, a flat rate scheme allows you to just account for the VAT on the taxable supplies you make and not make a return for the VAT you have incurred. A lower amount is remitted to HMRC which takes into account VAT you may have suffered.

The scheme is only available if the estimated VAT turnover – excluding VAT – is less than £150,000 in the next 12 months.

Once on the scheme, a business can remain on it until their total business income exceeds £230,000.

There is a separate form to join the flat rate scheme, which can be found at http://www.hmrc.gov.uk/forms/vat600frs.pdf.

A list of the flat rate percentages is published by HMRC, but it is your responsibility to check this list on a regular basis as flat rates do change and you need to adjust to the new rate at the correct time.

One thing you may not know is that if you apply to use the flat rate scheme, you can have a 1% reduction on your flat rate for the first 12 months of the business applying VAT. For example, if you apply to become VAT registered effective 1 July 2018 and you apply for the flat rate scheme of 12.5% effective on that same date, you can apply 11.5% to your turnover until the day before the first anniversary of being VAT registered. So, all invoices up to 30 June 2019 can be paid over at 11.5% instead of 12.5%.

If the business did not start applying the flat rate scheme until 1 December, they could still only have the 1% reduction until 30 June. Of course, if the business waits a couple of years before applying for flat rate, then they cannot use the 1% discount as it has passed the first 12 months of VAT registration.

How does VAT work under the flat rate scheme?

You raise invoices to your customers and you add 20% VAT onto the invoice and declare it as VAT.

When it comes to the end of the quarter, add up the total that is on the invoices including the 20% VAT element and then apply the applicable flat rate to this amount. This then gives the amount to be paid over to HMRC as your VAT submission. No VAT can be recovered on purchases.

Hey look – you get to keep some of the money that you collected – woo hoo. It is only a good thing if your costs are not high, or your costs are mainly at a zero rate or VAT exempt. This is something that needs to be assessed before flat rate is applied for. The money you do get to keep becomes part of the business income and is taxed as such as income for income tax or corporation tax. Boo hoo.

This table shows invoices raised in the quarter, and the amount of VAT to be recorded and paid over on the VAT return.

	Net	VAT 20%	Gross	Flat rate 12.5%	Income gain	1st year	1st yr gain
Jan-19	400.00	80.00	480.00	60.00	20.00	55.20	24.80
Feb-19	900.00	180.00	1,080.00	135.00	45.00	124.20	55.80
Mar-19	3,200.00	640.00	3,840.00	480.00	160.00	441.60	198.40
	4,500.00	900.00	5,400.00	675.00	225.00	621.00	279.00

This works well provided you don't buy anything big or have lots of input VAT. The VAT man has made an allowance: if you do buy a piece of equipment that is priced over £2,000, you can reclaim the VAT on this.

The main problem now is that from 2017, the government introduced a limited cost trader rule, in that if you do not spend a certain amount on goods for your business (not services), then you must apply a flat rate of 16.5%. Once this is applied, there is no benefit in using the flat rate scheme, and you possibly could be losing out and end up paying more VAT than if you were on the standard scheme.

As musicians, actors and performers, there is no point in being on this scheme, so unless you don't mind losing VAT and want to keep to a simple scheme, ignore this scheme, and you have wasted 10 minutes reading all this. Sorry.

What is the cash accounting scheme?

On the standard rate scheme, you need to account for VAT based on the date that the invoice was raised (or tax point) and also the date you committed to a purchase – so the date the invoice to you was dated or received is significantly different. This may seem unfair as you could raise an invoice in the last few days of the VAT quarter, but you won't get paid for six weeks. You need to have the cash in the bank to pay over the VAT before you have received it.

Cash accounting allows the business to set the tax point date of the date that their invoices were paid, and the date that they paid suppliers. Your turnover must be less than £1.35m and the scheme can be used until the business turnover reaches £1.6m.

Annual VAT accounting

There is the other extreme that is available if your turnover is less than £1.35m and that is an annual scheme. Don't get excited now. You make nine monthly payments (or three quarterly payments) to HMRC, complete one annual return and then the balancing amount is calculated, and the final payment or refund is made at the end of the year. The scheme can be used until the business turnover reaches £1.6m.

Story:

A client ran a rock and blues band and decided that it was too much for him to do his accounts and tax at the end of the year. I reviewed his prior year records and discovered that he was above the VAT threshold. Having warned the client that this may be a problem, HMRC VAT did write to the client as they noticed his self-assessment tax return showed turnover above the threshold and wanted to know why he hadn't registered for VAT.

Panic – how does a cash-based business deal with this when dealing with door takings and merchandise sales?

We came up with a plan going forward, but using his diary as a record of where they played and the money they took, we completed a UK v Europe gig list, and it turned out the UK-only gig and merchandise sales meant they were below the VAT registration threshold and did not have to be registered, but it could have been a whole heap of pain.

Of course, we are here to help you, so if you get stuck, book a call in with us at https://performanceaccountancy.youcanbook.me/.

Things you need to do

- ☐ Keep a running 12-month list of your income whether on the cash basis or normal accounting basis.

- ☐ Split that income into UK based and overseas so you know if you are near the UK threshold.

- ☐ If you get close to the threshold, review the best scheme for you and your business.

- ☐ Remember if you are a sole trader, it affects you and all your self-employed businesses (if you have more than one).

- ☐ Complete the VAT1 form or get some professional help.

CHAPTER 20:

Insurance

Now, this may seem like a strange thing to cover in this book, but every self-employed person needs to have insurance to help protect themselves. I'm not suggesting health insurance or life insurance, although both would be good but not tax deductible, but I am talking about public liability insurance. If something goes wrong, and it's potentially your fault, then hopefully you will be covered.

For example, if you're a singer and you often go into care homes and sing for the elderly, if one of them starts to wander and trips over your power lead, or your microphone lead, then well who's to blame? You could say the care home as they were not supervising the residents or providing you with adequate safe facilities, but more often than not, it'll be down to you as it is your equipment and your lookout for safety provision. Harsh, but there you go.

It's the same thing with anything in the public, but also if you teach from your own home. What if your pupil tripped over a loose rug and cracked their head on the coffee table?

Have you thought also about the home insurance side for teaching at home, because, well, it's possible that you might invite anyone into your home to teach them. A pupil could steal things, break things, etc. and how would you deal with that? How would you explain this on your home insurance claim if they don't know this is what you do? Yes, there are bound to be premiums to pay but it is best to be safe than sorry.

Of course, if you are a member of Equity, the Musicians' Union or ISM, part of their benefits package covers public liability insurance. So check out if it's worth joining one of them to get this covered.

Some insurance can be claimed through your tax return.

Things you need to do

☐   Do you know what insurance you need?

☐   Are your insurance needs covered by union membership?

☐   At the very minimum, get public liability insurance.

SECTION 5:

What's this limited company stuff?

CHAPTER 21:

Setting up a business –
self-employed v limited company

Some of this is a recap on what we have said before, but it is important to note if you are not sure about being a limited company, or if you could work as a sole trader/self-employed person.

What is a business? This is always an interesting question. You would be classed as being in business if you are selling goods and/or services on a regular basis, be it online, car boot sales, classified ads etc. You are classed as trading if you are trying to sell for a profit, selling on a regular basis, earn commission from selling goods for other people or if you are paid for a service you provide. However, you are probably not trading if you sell some unwanted items occasionally.

Having established you are in business, there are several ways you can carry on this business and this paper looks at the two most popular methods – self-employed/sole trader, or as a limited company.

Being a sole trader

Often when people start up in business, this is the easiest and logical format to start off with. It is simple to understand and should be simple to administer. However, you should get yourself into good business practices with things like separate business accounts and adequate paperwork to distinguish between yourself and your business. To be a sole trader in the UK, you must have a National Insurance number and be registered for self-assessment with HMRC.

Legally, there is no distinction between yourself and the business. You don't have to have a separate business bank account, but a separate account is an advisable business step. All the debts of the business are your own debt and if there are not enough business assets to cover your debts, then you are personally liable and personal assets can be used to pay the debts. This includes your home.

> **WARNING**: I stated above that legally you don't have to have a business bank account as a sole trader, BUT banks are getting a bit sniffy with personal bank accounts having lots of transactions going through them, and in the bank's terms and conditions, they may state that the accounts cannot be used for business. So please check this out as the bank could close down a personal account used for business.

In looking at taxation, you pay income tax on your taxable profit, but you do get a personal allowance to offset against the profit. Class 2 National Insurance has to be paid of a certain amount per week which is a personal cost and not a business cost, and at the end of the tax year, you will then be assessed for Class 4 National Insurance based on profit. Therefore, if your profit is less than your personal allowance, there will be no income tax to pay, but you may have to pay Class 4 National Insurance as they are set at different levels at the moment.

The good news is that all the profit you make and the cash you have is yours to do with as you please – provided you make provision for paying your tax bill by 31 January (and possibly 31 July if you need to make a payment on account). You may want to consider incorporation when your profits are over

£25,000 per year consistently. If you have profits that are above the 20% income tax threshold, then becoming a company is probably a no-brainer as company tax is 20% up to £300,000.

Benefits of being a sole trader:

- ♫ You are completely in control.

- ♫ You get to keep all your profit after tax. You don't have to share it with anybody.

- ♫ You are able to provide a personal service with local roots and become the specialist in the local area.

- ♫ You can make decisions quickly without necessarily having to involve others. This can greatly benefit your customers.

- ♫ All data on the business is kept private as there is no public record on the details of the person or the business unless you make it so.

Disadvantages of being a sole trader:

- ♫ You have to find your own work.

- ♫ As mentioned before, you have sole liability for your debts and the liability is unlimited.

- ♫ As the decisions are solely the responsibility of the sole trader, it is up to them to make the business a success. There is nobody else to help ease the pain.

- ♫ Sole traders often find it hard to raise finance to fund their business so may struggle to expand.

♪ You may not be able to buy in bulk on more favourable terms, therefore becoming more expensive to customers.

Self-Employed	Limited Company
Register with HMRC as Self-Employed	Create a company with Companies House including a registered office and director's service office
Register for Self Assessment	Register with HMRC for corporate tax
Business name for your own use	Business name is public
Online portal for yearly tax return	Specialise software for corporate tax returns
	Adhere to the Companies Act with strict fines
Separate bank account ideal	Separate bank account legally required
Simple form accounting system	Accounting is more complicated
Easy to take money out of the business	Hard to take money out of the business
20%/40%/45% income tax to pay	19% corporate tax. Implications for income tax
Personal allowance for individuals	No personal allowance for a company

Setting up as a sole trader

Sole traders must register with HMRC as being self-employed. You must ensure that you are registered no later than 5 October following the end of the tax year you started to trade. For example you started your business on 9 December 2018, so you have to have registered as self-employed by 5 October 2019. You will need to complete the self-employment section of the self-assessment tax return for the tax year 2018/2019.

You can give your business a name or trade as your own name. There are certain rules about this, but the main ones are that you do not have the word "limited" in the name in any form, suggest a connection to a government office, be similar to a registered trademark, include offensive names, and anything that is a sensitive word – this can include the word "bank". The sensitive names or expressions have to be cleared by a registered body, for example the Financial Conduct Authority, if you do use the word "bank" in your business name.

Setting up as a sole trader/self-employed person was covered in Chapter 4 as well as the bookkeeping requirements of being in business for yourself in Chapter 8.

You may need to register for VAT if your turnover goes over a certain amount (www.gov.uk/vat-registration). If this happens, there are various schemes available for completing VAT returns. An overview of VAT is in Chapter 19. This may mean monthly, quarterly or yearly returns for the VAT paperwork and monthly or quarterly payment of VAT due.

As I mentioned earlier, a self-assessment tax return needs to be completed and filed at HMRC by 31 October if doing so on paper or 31 January if completing an online form. This is discussed in Chapter 22, and there is a training course available if you'd rather do the tax return yourself, as many people feel they cannot afford an accountant. The training course we offer is located here: https://performanceaccountancy.co.uk/training-courses/.

Becoming a limited company

Incorporating your business can be useful at saving tax and utilising low rates of corporation tax (see https://performanceaccountancy.co.uk/rates/) and enabling the use of dividends. However, it does depend on how much profit you are likely to earn as for low profit businesses, it is often more tax efficient remaining as a sole trader. Of course, there are other reasons why you may wish your business to be a company and not have sole trader status.

"A limited company is an organisation that you can set up to run your business – it's responsible in its own right for everything it does and its finances are separate to your personal finances. Any profit it makes is owned by the company, after it pays corporation tax. The company can then share its profits." This is the definition per the government website.

There are two forms of company:

- ♪ Public Limited Companies (PLC) – must have at least two shareholders and at least £50,000 worth of shares issued. Often the shares are publicly traded.

- ♪ Private Limited Companies (Ltd) – can be set up with one member and any value of issued shares. These shares cannot be sold publicly.

For the rest of this section, I am only dealing with private limited companies.

Yes, there MAY be tax advantages to becoming a company depending on the income/profit level of the company, but there are thresholds of effectiveness and subsequent budgets may change it. If being a company is marginal for tax purposes at the moment, then it is not a good enough reason. Limited liability may come into play; for example, a divorce is on the cards and you want to limit access to funds, or you may just want the kudos of being a company. Some bigger companies only want to trade with other companies as the perception of being a company is better than being a sole trader. BUT you have to be ready for it or have people around you that can deal with all the accounting and admin headaches.

The great thing about a company is that the people that set it up keep their personal assets and wealth away from the company. It is only the shareholders that take any risk to the amount they have invested which may only be £1 for one share. A company is its own legal entity.

Benefits of being a limited company

- ♪ Limited liability as mentioned above. The company is its own legal entity and therefore protects the people operating in it – unless it is proved to be fraudulent or have illegal activities taking place.

♫ A limited company gives a comfort blanket to people investing in the company.

♫ Lower rate of taxation than a sole trader once the sole trader reaches the higher rate tax bracket.

♫ It allows a better tax regime for the shareholders for earning money as dividends can be paid.

♫ You are still able to claim a mileage allowance from the company via an expense report as well as a use of home charge.

♫ Usually the directors are the shareholders meaning decisions can be made fairly quickly and documented.

♫ Having a limited company secures the name so even if it is not ready to start to trade, nobody else can use the name. However, it does not give trademark protection.

♫ Doing business with other limited companies may be easier as they are seen to be more trustworthy.

Disadvantages of being a company

♫ It costs £15 to set up a company and each year you have to do an annual confirmation statement which notes any changes to the structure of the company and that costs £13 each year.

♫ There are strict rules and laws that need to be followed. This includes producing company accounts including a balance sheet (sole traders don't have to do this) and various notes to the accounts. This can be time consuming and costs money as it is something that you tend to get an accountant to do.

♫ There is no personal allowance for a company with regards to tax, so every penny of profit is taxed at the prevailing rate.

♫ There must be a distinction between the company and the people that run the business. You cannot just take money from a company bank account because you need it. You can only really take cash out of the business by using expenses, salary and dividends. If you take a director's loan and do not pay it back, there are legal and tax implications.

♫ The financial affairs of the business are public knowledge.

♫ Unless a privacy package is used, the director's home address or operating address is a matter of public record. To keep a registered office and director's service address out of the public record costs a certain amount each year.

But before I go into the things you need to know about running a company from the finance and administration side, have a think about whether this is a new venture to you. Often, the first year or two of a business makes a loss or very little profit. If this is the case, and you don't need to be a limited company, then you may be able to utilise any losses against other personal income in the year incurred, or small profits used against your personal allowance. Losses in a new company can only be used in the company going forward and are therefore locked into the company. Once the business becomes profitable and to a level it is tax efficient to be a company, then create the company and transfer the business.

The things you need to know but may not be told

Director's responsibilities – may be subject to criminal law

I thought I would start with the scary one. Being a director has responsibilities that are written into company law, and therefore if you don't do things properly or on time, you may be committing a criminal offence. It's always considered that company law is a bit weak and nobody takes it too seriously, but if you submit your accounts and other paperwork late, then it is a criminal offence. The worrying thing is that if you fail to keep proper accounting/business records, it's also a criminal offence.

The company money is not yours

You may be the only director and the only shareholder, but the company and you are two separate legal entities, so although you are earning money for the company, that money belongs to the company. You cannot just dip your hand into the company bank account if you run short of money personally. It's theft. Any money from the company to your personal bank account (or being used for personal affairs) must be backed up by the proper paperwork – payroll, expenses, dividends. Anything else is a loan from the company which has to repaid in full otherwise there are tax consequences for you personally and the company. So – in other words – don't do it.

Is it really limited liability?

That is one of the big attractions of being a limited company in that it is the company that is liable and not the directors and shareholders. But – think again. There are occasions where creditors can get to you, especially if it is considered that the company is wrongfully trading. A bank will often ask for a personal guarantee if they lend to the company.

Hidden accounting costs

You are likely to pay more for your accountant because there is a lot more to do with regards to the accounts and tax returns, along with director loans, dividend issues, changes in company laws and accounting regulations that have to be applied. Although the accountant won't be liable for unknown errors, they will do their best to advise you of things that they become aware of. If you don't use an accountant as a sole trader, you may want to consider one as a company. With the ability to file online with Companies House and HMRC, you can do all the filings required without the need for an accountant.

Proper accounting records

We've already stated that it is a criminal offence to not keep proper accounting records. So if you have the idea of just shoving the receipts into a drawer or shoebox, then think again. A company needs to keep more detailed records, so you really need some form of accounting system, and if the digital reporting comes about, good luck if you don't have something.

The bank

The number of people who I talk to who have set up their company, and are running their company with invoices etc, but running the bank through a personal bank account. No no no no NO. You and the company are two different legal entities. The earmarked company money is not yours. This makes it a loan from the company to you – what a nightmare. Bite the bullet – make an appointment with your business bank manager, take your incorporation certificate and other ID to that meeting and set up a company bank account. You may be lucky and get a year's free banking, but the bank fees are an allowable expense for the company, so sorry – suck it up.

Expenses of the company

Gone are the "round sum" expenses you would put through as a self-employed person; it's time to get real with proper expenses with back-up. And you can forget about the working from home allowance you used to get as a sole trader – different rules apply for a company and its employees. If you are operating the company correctly, you as a director should be on the payroll.

Pre-incorporation costs

Some costs incurred would be allowable to bring into the company when it first starts to trade, but they have to be proven to be for the company, and if bringing in items that had use before, they can only be brought in at a reduced value, for example a computer purchased six months before the company was formed, but that is going to be used in the company, needs to have its value reduced to recognise its use before being a company asset. Expenses incurred wholly and exclusively in the course of setting up the business for which the company was later formed can be reclaimed.

Typical pre-formation expenses include: internet and domain name fees, computer equipment and software, accountancy and other professional fees, and travel costs. Other costs MAY be allowable and it is assumed they were incurred on the first day of trade. The actual fee for creating the company is not allowable against corporation tax, although it is a cost of the business. Sorry.

Number of shares

It is up to you how many shares you have and the value of the shares. You could have one share valued at £1, or 100 shares valued at £0.01 or valued at £1, £10 etc. But think about growth. If you want to bring on investors, if you only have one share, then you need to jump through a few Companies House hoops to issue more shares. If you build flexibility at the beginning, then you can do transfers. Be careful of your decimal point. One client set up his company with one share with a value of £0.001. It got sorted out, but gave the wrong impression to the outside world.

What documents have to be filed and when?

If you don't file the right documents at the correct time/in the correct time limits, you can discover that your company no longer exists, and your company bank account is frozen. Ouchie. How can this happen? It happens very, very easily and frequently.

You may have set up a company in July 2016, filed dormant accounts in August 2017, carried on in business through 2018 and 2019 thinking you were operating as a company, not realising that as you had not filed your annual confirmation statement that your company had been struck off way back in February 2018. What a nightmare to try and unpick. All because you didn't know what had to be done when and thinking that filing your annual accounts was the same as filing your annual confirmation statement. Of course, you get the other way round where people file their annual confirmation statement but don't bother filing their annual accounts and tax return as they are dormant or took advice from the man in the pub, and then the fines start racking up. One client we had did this, which meant that the eight months of fines was more than the turnover for the year.

Always keep a record of your own company dates and when things need to be filed. Don't rely on your accountant for everything.

Setting up as a limited company

All companies must be registered at Companies House. In order to do this, you need the following:

♫ The planned company name and the registered address.

♫ One director (there is not a requirement now for a company secretary).

♫ The name and address of each director if more than one (a director's service address and home address are required).

♫ Details of the company's shares and who the shareholder/s will be and their address/es.

♫ The rules on how the company is to be run – the Articles of Association. For most companies, the model set is adopted (see http://bit.ly/modelarts).

♫ An online payment method.

For the company name, there are certain rules which are the same as setting up as a sole trader, so as a reminder, the name should not suggest a connection to a government office, be similar to another company, be similar to a registered trademark, contain offensive names, and any words that are sensitive, which can include the word "bank". The sensitive names or expressions have to be cleared by a registered body, for example the Financial Conduct Authority.

Once the above is known, go to Companies House (http://bit.ly/co-set-up) in order to start to register a company. You will need to register as a new customer.

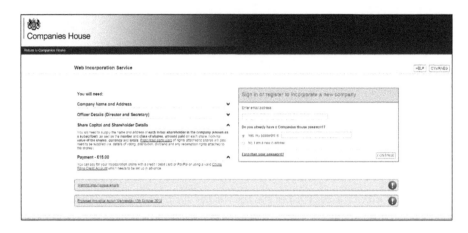

It is then a case of completing the boxes with the information you already know.

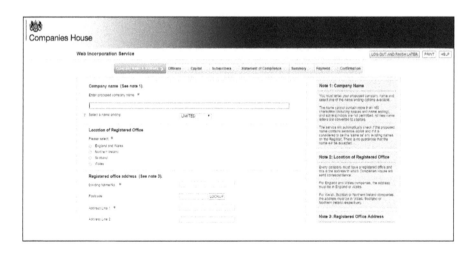

The £13 fee can be paid by PayPal, debit or credit card. It takes up to 48 hours to obtain confirmation that the company has been registered.

Another option is to use a formation company. This can cost a lot more than £13 as the basic set-up, but you can use their office as the company's registered office as well as the director's serviced office. This works well as then personal details are outside the public record. Some formation companies claim to have your company set up and ready in three hours.

Postal applications can take 8 to 10 days and cost £40. Postal applications can be same day, but the cost with Companies House direct is £100.

The directors are legally responsible for the company.

The shareholders are the owners of the company and have certain rights.

HMRC will send the unique tax reference to the company's registered office a few days after it has been registered at Companies House. Within three months of starting up in business, information must be given to HMRC and they will then work out when corporation tax will be payable. The form for this is called CT41G which should be sent to you when the company is registered; the most important information is when you started to trade. This is doing anything in the company's name such as buying materials, renting premises etc.

The final "must do" to set up the company is to set up a business bank account in the name of the company. Some banks offer new business accounts 12 to 18 months' free banking. What must be remembered is that business accounts have fees for every transaction that goes through the account – every cheque written, deposit made, and monthly charges just to have an account with them. It may be worth joining something like the FSB (www.fsb.org.uk) as they offer free banking with the Co-op, so the £150 fee could be saved on bank charges and you get all the other benefits of membership thrown in.

Other things to be done

Company stationery must bear the full name of the company with Limited or Ltd after it, the registered company number and the registered address. This includes invoices, purchase orders, letters, compliment slips, contracts etc and anything else that can be used to bind a company.

You may want the company to register for VAT from the outset. There is a compulsory threshold for registration, but voluntary registration can take place. VAT is explained in Chapter 19.

You don't have to have your books and accounts reviewed and audited by an accountant. Provided you have the correct software, you can create and file your own accounts at HMRC and Companies House. A company only needs to be audited if they meet two of three of the following:

- ♫ Their turnover is over £6.5m.
- ♫ Assets are valued at over £3.26m.
- ♫ They have 51 or more employees.

The books and records must be maintained on a regular basis as they can be requested and reviewed by HMRC whenever they like. They must be fit and properly maintained. You don't have to have an accounting system; Excel works just fine, but things need to be orderly and well maintained. Invest in some files, a hole punch and a printer/scanner. Records must be kept for six years. Records can be electronically stored but it must be possible to obtain a clear image (back and front if applicable). HMRC can go back 20 years if they feel there has been negligence. This is the same for a company and sole trader. There are further notes on this in Chapter 8, on bookkeeping records.

Although you don't need to have an external accountant set up for the company, you may decide to appoint one as your tax agent to deal with all the accounting and tax work on your behalf. An authorisation form needs to be completed, signed and sent to HMRC. This does not absolve you of your responsibility of properly accounting and doing tax returns. The form can be found at: www.hmrc.gov.uk/forms/64-8.pdf.

Close to your heart will be how you can pay the directors. In the main it is:

- ♫ Via salary – You need a PAYE scheme set up if you are going to pay yourself via a salary. You can pay up to £702 per month (at the time of writing in 2018) without tax and NI issues. You can do this online at the HMRC website using the payroll tool kit. This is called "HMRC Basic PAYE Tools" and can be found at https://www.gov.uk/basic-paye-tools. Alternatively, you can outsource it at a cost of approximately £25+VAT a month to a payroll provider. I never do payroll and always outsource it. There is guidance about setting up employing people in Chapter 29.

♫ Dividends can be paid but you as an individual will need to pay tax on them and the amount depends on if you are a 20%, 40% or 45% taxpayer.

♫ If you have expenses that the company should pay you for, then raise an expense report from yourself and this becomes an accounting record for the company. Based on this, the company can pay you back for these costs.

♫ Director's loan – Don't do it. All sorts of accounting and tax implications come along with this.

Of course, you may set up a company and not plan to use it for a while. That means the company is dormant. Within three months, this form needs to be sent back to say that the company is dormant which will mean HMRC will not expect returns. However, you will still need to file dormant accounts with HMRC.

Partnerships, private unlimited companies and private companies limited by guarantee are other set-up options for business, but they have been ignored for the purpose of this book.

Things you need to do if setting up a limited company

☐ Decide on a name, registered office address, and who the shareholders are.

☐ Set the company up at Companies House.

☐ Open a limited company bank account.

☐ Register for corporation tax (if setting a company up online at Companies House, this is the next step).

☐ Ensure you get public liability and employers' insurance.

☐ Set up a payroll scheme and pay yourself each month.

☐ Look at an accounting system, be it Excel or something like Xero.

SECTION 6:

Here goes – the dreaded tax return

Myth:

I did a tax return last year; surely I don't have to do another one this year?

Fact:

Sadly it is a yearly task whilst you are self-employed or you have other sources of income or other reasons for needing to complete a return. HMRC will issue a letter to say if you have dropped out of the self-assessment obligation, but until that happens, you have to do one every year.

CHAPTER 22:

How to complete the UK Self Assessment tax return

Throughout this book so far you've learnt how to register as self-employed, you understand what the UK tax system is and know what the self-assessment tax return does. We've looked at your personal digital account, what your timelines are, and we've even looked at how you invoice people and what expenses you can actually have against your self-employment.

What I haven't touched on is how to complete the self-assessment tax return. Now, as you are probably aware by now, the tax year starts on 6 April and finishes on 5 April. The tax return for the year then has to be filed online by 31 January following that year. Let's take tax year 2019/2020. We're going to go from 6 April 2019 to 5 April 2020. That means your tax return has to be filed by 31 January 2021. It gives you 12 months of the tax year to pull your paperwork together and then at the moment another 10 months before you actually have to do the filing. This is obviously ignoring any future plans for making tax digital and quarterly reporting.

Anyone can do a self-assessment tax return

Self-assessment isn't just for self-employed people. Everyone who has to complete a tax return must do so, even if there's nothing to pay. You could be charged a penalty if you don't.

Accountants would like you to think that completing the tax return is quite a complicated process. Well, it isn't if you know what you're doing, which is why we're doing this book and creating training courses, so if you know what you're doing, and you have an idea what your income and expenses are as well as all the other items for the return, then it could be a doddle. Sometimes tax is simple, but not in cases where you have things like foreign income popping in or capital gains tax, the latter of which is not covered in this book.

Completing your own tax return once a year is quite a big responsibility and if you only do it once a year you're bound to forget what you've done the previous year and it can be quite hard to go about getting things right. Rules change, new things get introduced, for example the low-income threshold for self-employed and property income, and rates may not stay the same year on year. As an individual, how do you keep up with it all? Sometimes getting help with your accounts and tax returns is a must. Big firms often cost way too much money and small firms might not have the experience of dealing with your particular industry. Most accountants charge by the hour, so are you really sure what your bill will be? However, it could be a case of you just needing someone to review your tax return or just go through various questions.

So the time comes to complete your self-assessment tax return. What do you need to do? Well, you've opened the Government Gateway account so hopefully you will still remember your login and have your password somewhere. It's time to collect all the documents that you need. The best thing is to make sure you've got those documents before you even start looking at the tax return. We've already mentioned things like bookkeeping records, keeping a log of your income, and a log of your expenses. If you have these at hand, it will make everything so much simpler.

Once you've registered and activated the online service, you're ready to complete your first self-assessment tax return. All income has to be included when you complete your tax return, so you'll need your records. These are some of the things you might need, but it is not an exhaustive list. A typical performer checklist can be found at the end of this chapter.

Employment

> P45   P60   P11D
> Student loan statement
> Notice of coding
> Employment expenses

Pension income

> State pension letter
> Personal pension P60
> Other taxable benefits

Self-employment

> Bookkeeping records
> Completed bookkeeping workbooks

Property income

> Rent a room income
> Rental income accounts
> Property details

Before you fill in your tax return you'll be asked to tell HMRC a bit about you. You must make an entry at every box with a red star beside it. The screens are very user friendly and help you through the process.

Errors can easily happen, but these are flagged up as you try to save the screen and move on. The main error is dates. Date must be in the format of dd/mm/yyyy, so four digits for the year, whereas we are so used to just putting two. In the next section you can tailor your return as to what income and costs are relevant to your tax return. You answer a series of yes/no questions to ensure that you only fill in what you need to.

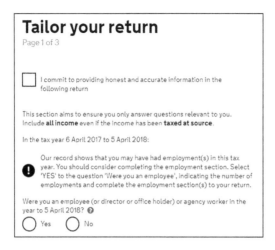

If you're unsure about a question, select the question mark at the side. You'll then find some guidance notes about what you need to do. Every time you use the "Next" button, what you've entered is saved. You don't have to complete it all in one go. You can leave the return at any time and come back to it later. That's helpful if you don't have everything to hand.

Here is an example of what you get when you click the question mark:

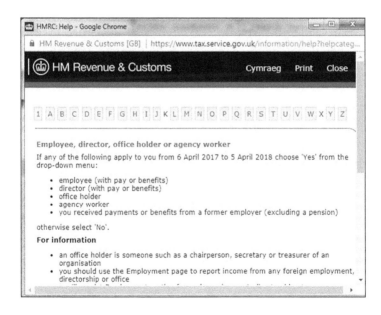

You can use the "Save" button to save your information up to that point. Then the "Check your progress" bar helps you to see how much you've completed and how much you must still do. The bar at the top of the screen moves along as you fill out the return. It can be depressing when it seems to be stuck at 4%, but it stays at that level until you have completed all the income and cost data and moves off that low percentage as you progress through the rest of the main sections.

Self-employed income

With regard to your self-employed income, you must record all income received as part of your self-employment. If you are paid a fee plus expenses, then you need to declare the full amount including those expenses. It could be a case of you getting a fee plus per diem and that per diem needs to be declared as income.

If you have received **income from abroad** for your self-employment, you need to record the gross fee you have earned, which is not necessarily the amount you physically received due to withholding tax and other local taxes, but we've already covered that in Chapter 14. You may have received a one-off fee in cash, and yes, cash fees also have to be accounted for. No matter how the money's come in, cash, cheque, bank transfer, PayPal or any other method, etc, it needs to be in your income.

We've already mentioned that the basis of your income needs to be when you earned it, unless you are doing the cash basis. In other words, even if you did a gig on 31 March and you weren't paid for it until 15 May that 31 March gig should be in your income for the tax year. Of course, some people have special years and they decide they want to do their tax and accounts to a different year end. Popular days are 30 April or 31 August. A lot of teachers do it to August so they keep to the school year. It does get very confusing, so why bother making your life a bit of a misery? Just stick to 31 March or 5 April as being the end of your accounting year for your tax return.

One thing you need to be wary of is sometimes you might have a PAYE job and you also might work for the same firm or the same opera or orchestra on a self-employed basis. You need to make sure that for the self-employed section of the tax return you only include items that were for your self-employment. Do not include any PAYE income or any PAYE expenses you might have incurred.

If you are still at university, one of the greatest misconceptions regarding income tax is that you don't have to register or pay income tax until you leave higher education. Well, that's not correct. There are no age limits for income tax. Students have the same tax-free personal allowance as anyone else, and if you start to earn self-employed or freelance fees while still at college you should have registered for self-employment with HMRC. You still get a personal allowance, so it might be the case that you just haven't earned enough to pay tax, but all students would have to pay tax.

A related point is that you may have received a **student bursary or a scholarship**. That's great – congratulations. Bursaries and scholarships are tax exempt so long as you are in full-time education at a college or a similar institution. They do not count as any part of your self-employment income. They do not have to be anywhere on your tax return. Woo hoo! But if you've won a prize at a music competition, they are generally regarded as being earned in the course of your self-employment and will be taxable. It's only if you win a prize before self-employment has started that it would not form part of your taxable income. Prizes awarded as a mark of public esteem rather than as part of a competition, well, they are tax exempt. So, know what competitions you have been entered for or you are entering and know what kind of income you might get as to whether it's taxable or not.

It is a different matter if you received an Arts Council grant, as sometimes it is taxable and sometimes it is not. It is best to speak to the Arts Council about the award as they have an agreement with HMRC as to what attracts tax. Please see this article: http://bit.ly/ACEGrantTax.

Going back to other income, your income can come from many sources, be it teaching where you receive money from pupils' parents or the pupils themselves, orchestral payments, money from a fixer, or you might actually have an agent who does agent statements for you. With the agent statements, you need to account for gross fee and any commission and VAT that the agent has charged you that is an allowable cost and goes into the cost section of your tax return. You do not put the net fee in as your turnover or income.

Income from employment

You may have income from a pay as you earn job or PAYE job. That is declared completely separately in the tax return. It is not part of your self-employment. What you have to ensure you have is the P45 if you left a paid job during the year or a P60 if you are still employed by that employer at the end of the tax year. What often happens if you have an agency job like doing promotions in a supermarket, or temping roles, an agency may not take you off the payroll and at the end of the year they might forget to issue a P60, so always make sure you make a note of who you have worked through and chase up for any P45s or P60s you think you should have. Of course, you can phone HMRC and ask them for the information, but they'd rather not have everybody do that. There will be a time when this information will be populated directly into your tax return but we have only seen it a few times.

Finally, with regard to income for self-employment, you might want to look at your bank statements and do a kind of mop-up. If there's any income you have received and you can't work out what it was for, you then need to investigate it. You don't need to worry about if Aunt Edna has given you a thousand pounds for a birthday present, or if your parents have supported you through the year; that is not taxable income. If you have a refund from Amazon or other types of shops, etc, that refund is not taxable, but if it's a refund for a business expense it needs to go into the expenses side but as a negative because obviously you've been refunded back the taxable expense.

Allowable expenses – again

You now have a list of your self-employed income and now it's the time to pull together the list of your self-employed costs. There is a whole chapter all about expenses and what is allowable and what isn't allowable, so I'm not going to go through it here again. You just need to refer to Chapter 11.

HMRC recognises that in order to earn money the self-employed person will incur expenses. It's accepted that income tax will be levied only on the net profits of the business, but that does not mean that every expense incurred in the course of freelance work will be allowable as a deduction. It has to be wholly and exclusively for business purposes. Again, refer to Chapter 11 all about expenses and if you have any questions you can always drop me a line, at info@performanceaccountancy.co.uk.

Whether an expense is tax deductible can only be determined by reference to statute law, decisions of the courts over the years, and HMRC's own guidance. The expenses are actually claimed against the income of the business and that's why they must be recorded properly. Some people are under the misconception that if they have costs then income tax is worked out on income and then costs are deducted from that tax calculation. That is completely incorrect. Allowable costs are deducted from your income and then tax is applied. I have had examples when people think they get their costs back from HMRC. Again, that is completely incorrect. Just because I might travel into London on the train doesn't mean to say HMRC is going to send me a cheque for £35.

It often happens that you just do not have receipts for something, for small sum expenses... Well, when there is no receipt HMRC will accept a kind of contemporary record as evidence. This might be an entry in a diary or a cashbook, but you should not rely on these or entries on a bank statement or a credit card statement as these can be ambiguous.

Just as a quick aside, if you happen to be VAT registered, the amounts you put into your self-assessment tax return are the amounts before VAT, so your fee income before VAT is charged. Your expenses will be the net amount. Again, before VAT is charged because you have already have gone through the whole process of payment and reclaim in the VAT process. If you are not VAT registered, then it won't affect your income, but please remember when you do your expenses it's the actual cost you have suffered that goes into your expense list.

Other income

You may have other forms of income outside PAYE and self-employment, depending on what you've done in the past. It doesn't go into the self-employment section, but you might have income from a state pension or a personal pension. It still goes through the tax return but in a separate section. Pension – even if it's paid as gross – is still taxable. If you earn over £50,000 as profit or any other income, then you might have to declare that on your tax return if you claim child benefit, because child benefit starts to get clawed back if yourself or your partner earns more than £50,000 in taxable income.

You have to include things like savings income, dividends, and some state benefits that are taxable also have to be on the tax return. You don't have to include sources of income that are already tax-free, such as money held in ISAs or premium bonds or even lottery wins. Money made from the occasional eBay or Etsy sale also does not have to be declared. That is not trading income. That's basically you just flogging off your personal items.

Some state benefits are taxable and need to be on the tax return. HMRC do publish a list of those that are taxable and those that are not. This list can be found here: www.gov.uk/income-tax/taxfree-and-taxable-state-benefits. It is worth checking each year. At the time of writing, the following are taxable:

State benefits that are taxable

The most common benefits that you pay Income Tax on are:

- the State Pension
- Jobseeker's Allowance (JSA)
- Carer's Allowance
- contribution-based Employment and Support Allowance (ESA)
- Incapacity Benefit (from the 29th week you get it)
- Bereavement Allowance
- pensions paid by the Industrial Death Benefit scheme
- Widowed Parent's Allowance
- Widow's pension

However, there are some little tweaks – for example the widow's pension – which is now the bereavement allowance. There is a bereavement support allowance (deaths after 6 April 2017) when a lump sum is paid plus 18 monthly payments. This support allowance is not taxable, but widow's pension and widowed parent's allowance is taxable. I have to admit, this whole area of allowances around death is highly confusing.

Property rental income

You might have property rental. Again, I've not covered this in the book, so that's a completely separate area. If you do rent out your property or you have lodgers, there is a potential tax liability for that. If you have sold an item of capital, there might be capital gains tax. What do I mean by an item of capital? Well, it could be a residential property that hasn't always been your primary residence. If you've been in the UK for a while, bought a property, then gone abroad for a couple of years and rented out that property, the property will be subject to capital gains tax. There is a separate allowance on capital gains tax. I don't plan to go into it in this book.

Let's say you've pulled together all your self-employment records and that part of your tax return is completed. You'll be able to review your National Insurance settings, and the return will then take you through some other sections to complete – for example contributions to charity. Charity giving can be a good way of increasing your 20% tax threshold. For more information, please refer to Chapter 18 on Gift Aid and charitable giving. National Insurance you have to pay is Class 4 National Insurance, at the moment 9% of your profits above a certain level, and you also have to pay a small amount of Class 2 National Insurance.

Student loan payments

Having worked out all the individual sections, it will then come to the part about the student loan. The tax return will ask if you have already paid anything towards your student loan in the tax year. This mainly comes through if you have a PAYE job and your employer has been deducted anything. If you are only self-employed, then this option won't be there, but when it comes to the calculation the student loan repayment will be calculated if you are over the threshold. Please see Chapter 16 regarding student loan payments.

As an annex at the end of this chapter, I have created a short checklist of the standard things you need to make sure you have ready to do your tax return. Make sure you go through the checklist to check you've got everything ticked off that you believe potentially is an item that needs to go into your tax return. This checklist does not cover everything for the tax return, but covers enough for an actor or musician. Always take time to double-check your return. Check all your numbers thoroughly before pressing the "Submit" button and please remember to press the "Submit" button. When doing online filing, you can save your tax return at any time and then go back to it at a later stage to do the double-checking. Make sure you print the calculation, or save it to your PC. Print the calculation of your tax and a copy of the tax return. Ideally, if you can do it in colour, great, or save the colour version to your PC. It is so much easier to read than the black and white version.

Payment on account

The final part is looking whether you have to make a payment on account. There is another chapter about payment on account (Chapter 27), but it can come as one heck of a shock when you realise you're paying income tax, two different types of National Insurance, repaying your student loan, and then you have a payment on account to make. If you can't make the payment when you think you're going to have to make it, you can call HMRC and they will set up a payment plan.

Summary

When you've filled in your return, you'll be asked to check that everything is correct. This shows a summary of what you filled in and confirms what you've said you don't need to fill in. At this stage you can go back and make changes. When you're sure everything is correct you can view your calculation. The online tax return works out how much you're due to pay. You can then save a copy of your return for your own records and the full calculation.

However, do remember to submit the return to HMRC. We often see people that have done the work, but just not hit that final button. You'll need your user ID and password to do this. Once you've submitted your return, you'll receive a message online to confirm that HMRC has received it. Always take a printout of the submission receipt (as well as downloading the calculation and the tax return earlier) so you have a reference to go back to in order to show you did submit it.

As I said before, the tax system can be complicated and taxpayers completing their own tax returns may unwittingly be declaring the wrong income or claiming for relief of items which they shouldn't have declared as tax deduction. HRMC might not actually get round to reviewing your tax return and just accept that it is called self-assessment for a reason, but they always pick random tax returns for review and investigation. It might be that they have been tipped off for something or it might literally just be a random selection. Keep your wits about you; ask questions of experts, not necessarily the man in the pub or the next player in the instrument section, because they might be just as confused as you are.

If you do want to seek an accountant, then make sure they understand the industry you're in. What you may have to provide for the accountant would be a written record of self-employed income and expenses, pay slips, invoices, P60s/P45s to vouch for amounts received, receipts or other evidence of expenses to be claimed, potentially bank statements to the main bank account used for business, and any other paperwork that might have a bearing on the tax computation such as foreign tax certificates, mortgage statements, agent statements, etc. If you do your own bookkeeping in a spreadsheet or an online system, then most accountants won't necessarily have to see the paperwork, although the first year that you're with an accountant they might like to have a look at it to get some comfort level that what you are putting through your tax return is actually correct.

There is a video training course available to show you how to complete your self-assessment tax return once you have logged into your personal tax account, and at the moment the course is based on the 2017/2018 tax year filing. The course can be located here https://performanceaccountancy.co.uk/training-courses/.

And now to make the completion of your tax return easier, a handy checklist follows of most of the things you are likely to require.

Checklist for performers

	✔	N / A
Employment		
P45		
P60		
P11D		
Student loan		
Notice of coding		
Employment expenses		
Pension income		
State Pension letter		
Personal pension P60		
Other taxable benefits		
Self-employment		
Bookkeeping records		
Completed bookkeeping workbooks		
Property income		
Rent a room income		
Rental income accounts		
Property details		
Investment income		
Bank interest statements		

	✔	N / A
PPI settlement details		
Dividend vouchers		
National Savings interest		
Overseas dividends		
Overseas income		

State benefits

Child Benefit details		
State benefits received		

Outgoings

Personal pension payments		
Annuity payments		
Gift Aid		
Student loan statement		

Capital transactions

NB – A small trader relief is available if self-employment income is less than £1,000 and if property income is less than £1,000. Let your accountants know if this is applicable to you.

CHAPTER 23:

What if you make a loss in your self-employment?

Myth:

In my acting career, I always make a loss which means I often get a refund.

Fact:

That may well be true, but too many years of losses, and HMRC may see it as a paid hobby so you may not be able to claim expenses, and just pay tax on the income. Under the new small trader allowance, you can earn up to £1,000 without it being on your tax return – provided this is the only self-employment you have.

Let's look at self-employed losses. When you first start up in business as a self-employed person the norm is you're going to make a loss. Nobody knows who you are, you have to establish yourself, you have to create your product and services. You have to go through any development phase for them and then begin testing the water. Your typical start-up cost of a self-employed person will be things like advertising, business cards, website, logos, if you think logos are important, networking, because that's often how you first get your contacts and often as performers lots of contacting agents, bookers and auditions.

Now, if you are a musician you might have to change to a much more professional instrument. You might have to buy new scores and learn additional music in the comfort of a soundproofed hire studio, just to get the first jobs coming through. It is typical that you make a loss in the very first year.

That's not too much of a problem; in the very first year you may have had some employment income; you might have been employed under PAYE, and that's great. You make a loss in your self-employment side and you can use something called sideways relief and offset the loss of your self-employment against your PAYE income. If you've paid any tax, potentially you can get some of that tax back. What you don't want to do, though, is use that self-employed loss to relieve against your PAYE income if you haven't actually reached the threshold of your personal allowance. If that is the case, then carry this loss forward.

One thing to note, though, if you have paid tax under a PAYE job and your PAYE income ends up being below the personal allowance, you will get that overpayment of tax back when you do your tax return. Don't waste losses if you are below the personal allowance.

You can offset your loss against any profits made in the same business up to four years after making that loss. It is only against profits of the same business, so if you suddenly decide to be a plumber having been an actor, then the offset of your loss can only be against the acting business and not the plumbing business. Also, when you carry the loss forward and you still have a PAYE job that you may be taxed on, you cannot offset the brought forward loss against that PAYE income. The sideways relief is only available in the year of the loss. Of course, if you make a loss in year two of your business, you could offset that against taxed PAYE income, and carry forward again the loss from the prior year.

There is a proviso when you do carry forward your losses: it is an all or nothing offset. You can't just say, "Oh, I've got X thousand pounds' worth of losses, I'll only offset part of it in order to make sure that year two, I'm below the personal allowance." It doesn't work like that; you have to offset all the loss if you carry forward.

There you go, losses in the first year – a great thing. Offset against any PAYE income or other income you might have, and/or carry it forward to next year, up to four years, until that loss is fully utilised.

CHAPTER 24:
Simple self-assessment

HMRC have recently launched what they call "Simple Assessment" tax returns. HMRC have pre-filled a lot of data already and all you need to do is to review it, and then say whether you are happy or not.

The affected taxpayers will receive a letter with a tax calculation showing their income from PAYE work, pensions, state benefits, savings interest and any employee benefits. If you believe that the information is incorrect, you as the taxpayer have 60 days to appeal it. However, normally, with a Self Assessment tax return, you actually get nine months to pull the information together and send it off to HMRC, so this 60 days is a major cut down in the time that you can appeal if you think the data is wrong, but that 60 days is also to cover getting the correct data.

Now, if you are reading this book, you probably are set up as self-employed, so you should not actually be sent a simple return as HMRC don't know what your income and allowable costs are to make such an assessment. If you do receive one, then they probably don't have you on their system as being self-employed, so you need to get that sorted quickly.

The simple assessment tax return was devised in order to save taxpayers the hassle of having to calculate exactly how much tax they owe. But how does HMRC get the data? Well, they have been launching, what I'm going to call a supercomputer, the Connect Platform. It draws on data from a whole host of government and corporate sources. For example, if you are a PAYE person, then your employer completes monthly payroll records. They're taking the information from the payroll system that the employer sends in and putting that through to your tax return.

The same goes if you get benefits from your employer: they must complete a P11D form, that goes off to the tax system, and so that extra section in your tax return is completed. It's the same now with bank interest. Banks provide HMRC with data on who actually receives interest on their bank accounts, and soon HMRC will also get information on dividends. When a publicly quoted company issues a dividend, HMRC will be able to get the data and allocate it to your personal tax account. That is a bit more complicated than the payroll returns, because I know when I've purchased shares in the past, I've certainly never given the company my National Insurance number, so how they're going to match that up, I'm not sure.

How they're going to match interest up is another concern for me. When I opened my bank account in the last century, I didn't give my bank my National Insurance number, so again I am not sure how I will be matched to interest received. It will be an interesting one to look at, and see how accurate the interest amounts are.

The simple tax returns that are coming out now are mainly for people whose income exceeds the personal allowance and for those that are drawing their state pension for the first time. However, I have seen clients that are nowhere near pension age with several different employments via payroll systems that have been issued them. If you do have a Simple self-assessment tax return, always check it.

CHAPTER 25:
Interest and dividends

Investment income is an area of the tax return that is frequently overlooked, probably because, as performers, we think that we don't get much investment income, so why should we worry about it? I understand that, and yes, it is true that there are certain thresholds, and providing your investment income doesn't go over those thresholds, it makes no difference whatsoever to your tax return. Again, why bother? Why make the effort to go through your monthly bank statements and find that 10p a month of interest from your savings account?

But, as mentioned in the previous chapter, the HMRC computer is collecting data from banks, so if you don't tick the box to say you've got investment income and they mark it to say, "Ooh, why hasn't that person ticked it?" they may then open an investigation into the tax return. You're just opening yourself to potentially a whole lot of pain if you don't record it properly on your tax return.

What do I mean by investment income? It's mainly interest from banks and building societies and dividends from companies. With interest from banks and building societies, you can earn up to, at the moment, £1,000 of savings interest before it gets taxed, providing you're a basic rate taxpayer. That is a lot of interest you need to get, given the interest rates are so low. Of course, if you have an ISA or a cash ISA all the interest is tax-free. That goes nowhere near your tax return. You can file the paperwork and forget about it.

When it comes to dividends, that is a different kettle of fish. Dividends can be from a publicly quoted company like British Gas, British Telecom, Rolls

Royce. They're ones that were floated by the government many, many years ago, and people bought shares into these. Your dividends from those companies are investment income. Or it could be that you own shares in a private company, and every so often that private company issues you a dividend. This is especially true if you are a director of your own company.

You can only earn a certain amount of dividend income before HMRC taxes you on it. It used to be free rein; you could earn as much as you like up to the 40% tax threshold. But they have slowly reduced that over the years. You haven't got to earn too much in dividends before you get taxed on it. Make a note of what companies you have dividends from, and list them on the worksheets in the tax return. The total only goes into the main tax return and that's all HMRC see. You need to keep your dividend vouchers showing money received.

Having said all that, you also get the potential of interest and dividends from an overseas company. Now you might bank with Santander. Santander at the moment is a Spanish company, so if you have any dividends from Santander, depending on what accounts you have, that actually is a foreign dividend. But you do have a threshold to go up to before you have to enter it in the foreign section. If you have less than £300 of foreign dividends, then it's just classed in the dividend section or the investment section of the tax return and you don't have to sit there and worry about tax deducted if any has been deducted, or declaring other interest. But again, with the Connect supercomputer that HMRC have built, they will be getting feeds from overseas banks for UK residents. Beware, that's another automatic feed that they will be supplying and checking as to whether you have declared it in your tax return. There are heavy fines for not declaring overseas income.

CHAPTER 26:
Enquiries into a tax return

So what happens after you've submitted your tax return? You submit your tax return, let's just say you're doing it online, and HMRC will process it. That means the figures actually in your tax return would just be input into the self-assessment computer system. At this stage, nothing is really happening apart from that it would do some automatic checks for obvious errors such as figures not adding up, etc. But the return will not actually be looked at closely.

If you've submitted the paper return before 31 October, you'll be sent a calculation of the tax due. If you've done it on the online system then you will receive confirmation that the return has been processed without need of correction, or another calculation will be posted indicating where the figures differ. Often this happens with Class 2 National Insurance if you haven't actually registered as self-employed; although you can do the tax return completing the self-employed section, it won't calculate the Class 2 so you might get a separate bill for Class 2 NI. Of course, that's whilst there is Class 2.

Adjustments also happen for the marriage allowance so the online system won't automatically offset the marriage allowance if it doesn't know to do it. If you haven't registered for the marriage allowance up front, it doesn't know to offset against it. If you're only doing the election on your tax returns, it will give the total figure to pay via the calculation sheet, and later on there will be an adjustment to your tax return, either reducing your allowance or increasing your allowance, depending on whether you are the giver or receiver of the marriage allowance.

There can be inquiries into your tax return. HMRC normally have 12 months from the submission of the form to open a formal enquiry (or 12 months from the end of the filing period). This is sometimes known as a Section 9A enquiry. The time limit can be longer than 12 months if the return is submitted late. Most inquiries are opened because the inspector knows, or suspects, something is wrong with the return but there are also a number of purely random inquiries each year. The inspector of taxes will never actually disclose whether the enquiry is random or whether they suspect something. So if they do open a Section 9 enquiry, HMRC will write to you and your accountant if you have one and set out their concerns by asking a series of questions or requesting documentary evidence of the numbers on the return. Once the enquiry is complete, the inspector will tell you if they want more tax, that nothing needs changing, or occasionally that you've paid too much tax.

Story:

Never ignore letters from HMRC as it can mount up to a whole pile of hurt later on. A person came to us as he was being chased by HMRC for unpaid self-employment tax. He has never been under self-assessment or self-employed and had only worked as a waiter in employed contracts. However, he moved about a bit and although employers were putting his new address on the payroll, HMRC letters never seemed to catch up. It turned out that yes, he did owe tax due to underpaid PAYE, but HMRC could not get any response from him (as he never received any letters), and so they turned the debit into self-employment tax owed which meant heavier penalties and interest charged. Yes, he owed the money, although he did not keep many payslips, but we were able to get the penalties and interest removed due to lack of notification.

If more tax is due, interest will be charged and an inspector may impose penalties, which can amount to up to 100% of the extra tax, and if there are offshore disclosures, up to 200% of the tax. If, when looking at your tax return for a particular year, the tax inspector finds a serious error and feels that it may have occurred in previous tax years, they are able to issue a discovery assessment for earlier years, even if that time period has passed. It comes back to making sure you keep your records in a safe, clean environment so that you know exactly where they are for six tax years plus the year you're in.

Things you need to do

☐ Don't panic.

☐ Look at what their query is about. It may just be a missing P45 not declared in your tax return.

☐ Make sure you have all information required.

☐ Don't write emotional letters to HMRC.

☐ If you feel you can easily answer the query, do so quickly as you normally only have a month to reply, but don't expect an immediate reply.

☐ Seek professional help if needed – this could be your professional body if a member of Equity, ISM or MU, or an accountant.

A long story

HMRC launched a working party to examine the letting industry as buy-to-let mortgages were on the increase but there was a gap between the number of landlords and number of people registering for self-assessment of rented income to the tune of about £500m. In autumn 2014 HMRC started the Let Property Campaign which gave landlords the opportunity to come forward and declare past undisclosed income.

At the same time, HMRC started to compel letting agents, via statutory notices, to inform them of what landlords they were collecting rents for. They had to hand over details of rents received on behalf of these landlords, and this went back to amounts paid in the tax year 2012/2013.

The statutory notices meant that they had 60 days to comply or face a penalty of £300 and up to £60 per day for continued failure to comply. There was also the possibility of a £3,000 penalty for inaccurate information provided. This now happens each year so you may see a fee on your rental remittance.

So now we move to Clive. He was always told that to save for his retirement he should put money in property – so from 2008, that's what he did. Money was saved for deposits and mortgages for the properties, then they were rented out without much work being done on them. All was well and a small portfolio built. Rented income just about covered mortgage costs (over the past decade rents went up twice as fast as rental income).

However, because of the HMRC activity, Clive received a letter from them saying they thought he owed tax going back to 2009/2010 and worked out a horrendous tax bill just based on income received as they had no other information or costs. (Mortgage companies at the moment don't have to feed information to HMRC, but the time will come, with the HMRC "Connect" supercomputer system, when they will have to.)

Clive had to go back to April 2009, find all his bank statements, remittances and invoices from the letting agent, mortgage statements and any other local invoices that are allowable costs such as insurance. Using this, we needed to create property accounts for the past seven years, plus look at any capital gains tax implications of finding the purchase costs (purchase price, stamp duty, renovation costs) and working out the sales costs and price. It's not just a case of dealing with the current year and then dealing with the rest later, but you also have to consider if any capital gains loss could be offset against any capital gains profits. No point in submitting the current year tax with a capital profit and forcing tax to be paid, where a loss could negate it.

The plus side of the story is that Clive set up a new bank account for each of the properties so most of the transactions going through were for that property and it was "easy" to build accounts per property. Of course, there are always occasions when there is money in the account that is used for other reasons.

The main issue was that Clive thought the whole mortgage payment could be offset against the rental income and not just the interest element. Where he thought he made a loss, it turned out that a couple of years he had made a profit so tax would be due. In the end, the true losses made offset the profits so the investigation was resolved with no tax to pay.

Things to learn

If you are going to be a landlord:

1. You must register with HMRC as a landlord in order to complete a self-assessment tax return.

2. We highly recommend having a bank account for each property, so the rent goes in it and the mortgage, plus other costs, come out.

3. Keep your remittance statements from the letting agent as you need to declare your gross rental income and costs if you let it through an agent.

4. If you rent it out yourself, keep a record book of money received and when.

5. Keep all invoices for allowable costs if paid for by you e.g. landlord's gas certificate, repairs and maintenance bills, utility bills during a void period, handover costs between tenancies etc.

6. Accounts are based on income received in the accounting year to 5/4/XX. If people pay in advance, the advance payment is counted in that year but the associated costs may fall in the following year. It is possible to treat the income as though received in the next year.

Ensure you get your tax return in on time. Rental profit counts towards student loan repayments!

CHAPTER 27:

What is this payment on account I have to make?

You now know that as a self-employed person, you've got to pay your tax bill by 31 January in the following year. However, what might come as a shock is if you actually have to make a payment on account. It comes as a shock because you might have budgeted for 20% of your profits to be income tax, 9% for your National Insurance, and a possible 9% student loan repayment, but all of a sudden there's this extra bit that comes in.

So, what is a payment on account? If you're a PAYE employee, then you'd be paying your tax and National Insurance on a monthly basis. As a self-employed person it can take up to 18 months to get the tax paid on money you've earned. Now, HMRC don't really like this because it plays havoc with their cash flow, et cetera. So, what they try and do then is say, "Right. I'm going to ask you to assume your business carries on as it has been in the year, so your tax bill will be the same for the following year, and you're going to make a payment of 50% upfront when you pay your tax bill."

To determine if you are caught by this, you look at your National Insurance and your income tax payable and then you go, "Okay, that's over £1,000." HMRC will add 50% of your liability to be paid on 31 January and another 50% to be paid on 31 July. If you're not expecting it, it can play havoc with your cash flow. But what they are good about, and I do use the term loosely, is that they do not include in the payment on account calculation any student loan payments and your Class 2 National Insurance.

Example:

Jeremy is a self-employed musician and does not have any other income. His fee income is £25,000, and his costs are £8,000 making his profit £17,000. After the personal allowance of £11,850, he is to pay income tax at 20% on £5,150. His tax bill looks like this:

Fee income	25,000
Costs	8,000
Profit	17,000
Personal Allowance	11,850
Taxable income	5,150
Tax @ 20%	1,030
Class 4 NI @ 9%	772
Class 2 NI flat fee	153
Tax bill	1,955
50% on account	901
Total to pay 31 jan	2,856
Amount to pay 31 July	901

So, be prepared that if you think you're going to have a tax bill of more than £1,000 you need to find an extra 50% to be paid by 31 January and 31 July. You've been warned.

However, you are able to reduce your payment on account. Woo hoo.

There is a little box in the tax return asking if you'd like to reduce this payment on account. What is it? What effect does it have? When can you use it?

A payment on account is you paying upfront for next year's tax bill. But if you know your tax bill (that would be your income tax and Class 4 National Insurance) is going to be lower than the last year, you can ask HMRC to reduce the payment on account. It may be that you're involved in a film project one year that paid you very well, but in the current year, nothing has turned up. You do need to have a reasonable grasp on your current numbers and know what you're likely to be earning for the rest of the year and the profit you'll have. In which case, you can make an estimate of your bill, divide it by two and ask for that to be your payment on account. You divide it by two as payment will be needed in January and July. Be aware though, if you reduce the payment on account too much and find your tax bill will be greater than that payment on account, you'll have to pay interest on the amount that you should have paid, and possibly a penalty charge, as you'll not have taken care on your records.

What I do often suggest to clients is that if they can make the payment on account for January, do so, but then ensure their tax return for the current year is done in April, May, or June, as then we'll know if another payment is needed in July, or if you can obtain a refund. You can do this reduction in payment on account either via your Government Gateway SA303, or directly in the tax return being filed.

SECTION 7:

Other useful information

CHAPTER 28:
HMRC Film and Production Unit

I know I said this book is for performers in the arts, music, media and entertainment sectors, and there will be a separate book for crew, but this is important as the film unit covers people like composers, musical directors and musical arrangers, plus I do have clients that appear front and back of camera, so I didn't want to miss them out.

This affects the "behind the scenes" people in the film and TV industry such as riggers, animators, art directors, composers, costume designers, camera operators, location managers, production buyers, special effects supervisors, etc, so if you don't work as a behind the scenes person, skip on ahead.

HMRC have a film industry unit and they issued a booklet called Film, Television and Production Industry Guidance Notes, and that provides guidance as to whether a person is employed or self-employed. If you are interested, it is in the HMRC archives here: http://bit.ly/FilmUnit. I have no idea why it is in the archives given it is a current document, but hey ho. As the title says, it is guidance, but it is followed quite closely and HMRC may contest your self-employment if the unit has your grade as employed.

So what is the problem of being treated as an employee? Well, you lose the benefit of being able to claim certain expenses which are set against your income which reduces your tax liability. Income tax will be paid as being an employee, and that will sort itself in the self-assessment tax return, but where it becomes an issue is that National Insurance will have been deducted and it's rather hard getting it refunded.

Now if the job you will be doing is not on the self-employed list, you MAY be able to obtain a "special authority letter" from the Film and Production Unit for a specific job, or a Lorimer letter (LP10) which can be used for several jobs. If you have one of these letters, then you are accepted as being self-employed and no PAYE or NI is deducted from your earnings. You just need to make sure you don't lose the bit of paper as it travels from job to job with you for three years and covers assignments of 10 days or fewer but they don't have to be consecutive days.

How do you get an LP10? Well I can tell you there is no online form and it is a letter with back-up information to be sent to the HMRC unit in Newcastle. They will require evidence to show that you have had sufficient short or daily contracts to qualify over the previous 12 months. I have heard that they expect around 25 of these, so if you are starting out, you probably won't be able to get an LP10. The second bit of evidence HMRC will require is that you are running a business with the associated risks of running a business. This is normally done via a questionnaire. A Lorimer letter cannot be backdated and will apply from the start of the month that it is granted.

Where things go a little strange is that HMRC have a seven-day rule, so if you work in film or TV, HMRC will allow you to be paid gross even if your grade is not on the self-employed list and the engagement is six days or less. The main difference is that it only applies to income tax, and you would still suffer National Insurance deduction, but the LP10 means no National Insurance will be deducted.

Just so you are aware, the seven days include weekends or breaks, but if you know you will be re-employed at a later date for the same company, the period extends beyond six days. Also if you are re-engaged frequently, then the seven-day rule is blown out.

Final word of warning: if you work on a short assignment but through an agency, the agency rules apply and you may be treated as employed.

CHAPTER 29:

Employing staff

I am going to start this by saying we are not employment lawyers, HR qualified or anything like that. This is what we have found when carrying out our business and helping clients. If you do plan on taking on staff on an employed basis, please seek proper advice. We can give you contact details of trusted HR people.

Congratulations that the business is doing so well that you need to employ somebody. It's said that the small businesses are the ones doing what they can to drive the economy forward.

Is it a case of you needing an extra pair of hands or is it a longer term view on structuring your business and introducing skills you don't have and would rather not outsource? Are you looking for a future manager and somebody that can cover for you when you are not available, or somebody more junior in an operational role? It may be a case of being able to outsource all the tasks you loathe to a VA service or having a bookkeeper/accountant to look after the recording of the finances.

If this is your first time employing someone, then you need to be set up as an employer and have a payroll scheme up and running. In order to do this, please refer to http://bit.ly/PA-EMPL as this takes you through the basic information you need to know.

An employee comes in many guises, and under the new HMRC rules of Real Time Information (RTI), all these people need to be set up on the payroll scheme and reported to HMRC:

- ♪ A full-time person
- ♪ A part-time person
- ♪ A casual worker
- ♪ A director

A distinction needs to be made as to whether they are an employee or self-employed. It all depends on the terms and conditions they have as a working relationship with you. This affects tax and National Insurance and if you need a scheme at all.

The main indicators of being an employee are:

- ♪ You can tell them what work to do, as well as how, where and when to do it.
- ♪ They have to do their work themselves.
- ♪ You can move the worker from task to task.
- ♪ They are contracted to work a set number of hours.
- ♪ They get a regular wage or salary, even if there is no work available.
- ♪ They have benefits such as paid leave or a pension as part of their contract.
- ♪ You pay them overtime pay or bonus payments.
- ♪ They manage anyone else who works for you.

Let's assume that the person/people you need to employ are going to be employees under your control. The self-employed test should be carried out at bit.ly/ESI-Aug18 to check if the person would be an employee or genuinely self-employed.

Managing staff and expectations is critical in case there may be disputes further down the line. This can be costly and specialist HR advice should always be sought.

From an accounting perspective

There is standard information that needs to be collected for an employee in order to create a payroll record for them and for them to be accepted as part of the HMRC Real Time Information reporting. The information that must be collected is:

- ♪ Full name
- ♪ Gender
- ♪ Date of birth
- ♪ Full address
- ♪ National Insurance Number
- ♪ Date employment started
- ♪ P45 showing their pay to date, tax to date, tax code plus any student loan deductions

Other information will be useful to hold such as passport number, visa number etc.

Clearly you will need to collect bank information if payment is to be made by bank transfer.

It does not make any difference if the person is only employed for a short period of time, if low paid, temporary or casual staff. Everybody employed must be recorded.

If you become an employer, there are certain responsibilities you need to take on board from a tax perspective:

- ♪ Calculating the correct PAYE and National Insurance to be deducted from the employee's pay as well as the employer's National Insurance.

- ♪ Paying over the tax and National Insurance on time to HMRC; it has to reach them by the 22nd of the month following the end of the pay period.

- ♪ Keeping accurate records and making sure they are up to date.

- ♪ Ensuring that you are compliant for any statutory sick pay, statutory maternity/paternity pay and other deductions such as student loans.

♪ Making sure that monthly reporting is sent to HMRC on or before the date you actually pay them their wages/salary.

♪ Being responsible for running the payroll system whether it is in-house, at a payroll bureau or using the HMRC tools.

Other considerations you need to take on board:

1. You must pay the legal national minimum wage per hour. It is a criminal offence not to. Sadly this does not apply to self-employed people. The current rates can be found at www.gov.uk/national-minimum-wage-rates.

2. You need to check that the person you are planning to take on is eligible for work in the UK. A National Insurance number does not guarantee legality to work. A copy of a passport is one of the checks and should be held in the employee file. The government offers a website for checking if somebody can work in the UK. The tool is found here: https://www.gov.uk/legal-right-work-uk. This will take you through questions about the person and ideally what documentary evidence you should have before you employ them. If checks are not carried out and it is deemed you have employed an illegal migrant, the civil penalty can be up to £10,000.

3. Do you work with vulnerable people or security, as you may need to sort out a DBS check (formerly known as a CRB check)?

4. Obtain employers' liability insurance which must be for at least £5m from an authorised insurer. This is often overlooked. You can be fined £2,500 for every day you are not properly insured. You can also be fined £1,000 if you do not display your Employers' Liability Certificate. Crumbs. The good news is that if you only employ a family member, or someone who is based abroad, you don't need employers' liability.

From a human resources point of view:

♪ Ensure that you use the right legal employment and HR forms and policies.

♪ Details of the job plus terms and conditions must be sent to the employee. The employee must have a written statement of employment if the employment is going to be greater than one month. It is not the same as an employment contract. It must be provided within the first two months of employment.

♪ The principal statement needs to cover:
  ♪ The business's name
  ♪ The employee's name, job title or a description of work and start date
  ♪ If a previous job counts towards a period of continuous employment, the date the period started
  ♪ How much and how often an employee will get paid
  ♪ Hours of work (and if employees will have to work Sundays, nights or overtime)
  ♪ Holiday entitlement (and if that includes public holidays)
  ♪ Where an employee will be working and whether they might have to relocate
  ♪ If an employee works in different places, where these will be and what the employer's address is

♪ The secondary statement needs to cover:
  ♪ How long a temporary job is expected to last if applicable
  ♪ The end date of a fixed-term contract if applicable
  ♪ Notice periods
  ♪ Collective agreements
  ♪ Pensions
  ♪ Who to go to with a grievance
  ♪ How to complain about how a grievance is handled
  ♪ How to complain about a disciplinary or dismissal decision

♫ The statement does not need to cover:
   ♫ Sick pay and procedures
   ♫ Disciplinary and dismissal procedures
   ♫ Grievance procedures

A template for the written statement can be found here: http://bit.ly/2CBJHG5.

Always set a clear expectation on the level of performance required. This is true for all types of employees including apprentices. For office/computer-based staff, maybe a social media policy (and monitoring) should be included in their terms of employment. We all know people like to use social media and rather than ban it, restrict its use by an honesty policy so staff know they can use it before and after work and in their lunch hour. Of course, you may have to monitor the situation. There should be a method of measuring overall job performance.

In order to protect yourself and your employee, have a trial or probationary period. The length of time will depend on the type of employee and possibly the work being done.

Set clear expectations on what is and what is not acceptable behaviour and have a written grievance and disciplinary procedure.

From 2012, it became law to offer a pension scheme for employees. This is known as auto-enrolment. As a small company, you will still need to offer a pension scheme.

HR is a whole different minefield but help can be found from the Federation of Small Businesses and independent HR groups, and ACAS have a small downloadable handbook for small businesses employing people.

Overall, if you are taking on an employee, expect a dip in profits as your income from the business now has to cover two salaries. Of course the idea of taking on somebody is to boost your income one way or another, but in the early stages, there will be a dip.

NB – You don't actually have to be in business to be an employer. If you employ domestic staff (what an old-fashioned term that is) like a nanny, housekeeper, cook, gardener etc. that are under your control in your home, then they need to be on a payroll scheme. And no, these people are not allowable costs of your business, so don't even think about going there. I've heard it before: "Without the nanny I could not go back to work and the tax man would have less money." Just don't go there.

CHAPTER 30:
How we can help you

I hope you've found the book useful to help you with your accounts and tax, but you may find that you need extra support.

If you'd like us to help you with your accounts, then it's a fairly easy process to follow. We chat to you about what you need from your accountant, for example a self-assessment tax return, full bookkeeping and accounting service plus year end compliance, workshop on processes, personal budgeting etc, and then draw up a quote for our services which will be valid for six weeks.

Should you decide that Performance Accountancy is right for you, then a whole process kicks off. You will need to resign from your current accountant and introduce them to us. The vast majority of accountants are familiar with the process and respond in a reasonable period of time (2 to 3 weeks), but there are times we may need you to give them a nudge. As long as you are up to date with fees, the outgoing accountant will not normally charge for this, although they may levy a small admin fee/postage to collect documents or post them out.

♪ We have a template which you can use in order to resign from your outgoing accountant and introduce us to them. That gives your outgoing accountant the approval to pass information to us.

♪ We will need to obtain various bits of information from you which is mainly via an online registration form.

♪ We complete the agent authorisation form on the HMRC website and HMRC post a letter to you with a code that you need to give to us to complete the process.

♪ We will write to your old accountants for the professional clearance and deal with any queries.

♪ Finally, we will need from you:

    ♪ The agreed quote for actual work

    ♪ A signed engagement letter

    ♪ Identity documentation for anti-money laundering requirements

    ♪ GoCardless details set up for payment

GLOSSARY OF TERMS

I have tried to make the book as free from jargon as possible, but I appreciate that this may not be the case, so hopefully here is a list of some words I may have used that need a bit of explaining.

Accruals basis of accounting – The effects of transactions and other events are recognised when they occur and recorded in the bookkeeping records.

AIA – Annual investment allowance – It relates to capital allowances on new purchases.

Assets / Capital – Those big bits of equipment/instruments that cost a lot of money and can last a few years, e.g. new instruments, laptop.

Expenses – The running costs of your business.

Gross income – Your fee income before any deductions.

PAYE – Pay as you earn. This is how employees get paid doing a "proper job" as my mother would say. Income tax and Class 1 National Insurance is taken from your pay (along with other deductions) before you receive your wage/salary.

Profit – Fee income less your expenses.

Revenue – Sales of your business or fee income before any expense deductions.

Self-employed – An individual owning and operating a business alone.

Sole trader – An individual owning and operating a business alone.

Turnover – Sales of your business or fee income before any expense deductions.

WDA – Writing down allowance – An amount that can be used as an expense on capital purchases that have not already been written off in prior years.

IS THIS THE END?

Nearly! I hope you "enjoyed" this book purchase. You did purchase it, didn't you!?

So what now?

The book should give you a great starting point in not only getting registered as self-employed but full knowledge of what records you need to keep, how you need to record the items and everything you need for your tax return.

However, this is only the start of your life in the business called show.

You will need to submit your tax return as a self-employed person. We have a training course that has been written to take you through all the main sections of the tax return. More details on our training course can be found here: https://performanceaccountancy.co.uk/training-courses/. Of course the training courses will have the same wit and charm that you have witnessed in the book.

You may decide that this is all too much for you and you'd like somebody to take it all away from you. Well, we can take away some of the stress and pain if you would like to come on board as a client. We speak openly (as I think you may have gathered by the book), and try really hard not to confuse you with accounting jargon. Most of the time the work is done by phone, Skype, email, Zoom or client portals, but we have been known to leave the office and venture to a location outside Bracknell – well, when I locate my passport anyway.

So if you want an accountant that understands your industry with many years of experience on stage and behind the scenes with a calculator, then get in touch. We do like to give personal service – ooh, that could sound so wrong – and we take care of the stuff that you loathe (tax and accounts, before you think of your mother-in-law), and we are good at it. We specialise in your area, and are the green apple in the sea of red apples so we stand apart from the others.

Please keep in touch. As you are a performer, you can join our Facebook group, and that way you'll be able to ask questions (not too personal, mind) and hopefully get a sensible answer: www.facebook.com/groups/PerformersTax.

Performance Accountancy
Tel: 01344 669084
Fax: 01344 449727
info@performanceaccountancy.co.uk
www.performanceaccountancy.co.uk
Diary Appointment: https://performanceaccountancy.youcanbook.me/

ABOUT THE AUTHOR

Louise obtained a Business Studies and Accounting honours degree and went on to train as a Chartered Accountant with Price Waterhouse, one of the top three accounting practices in the world. Her passion was always music and singing, so she studied voice privately for a couple of years.

The English National Opera started a training course called "The Knack", and she was one of the first students taking this year long training in 1995/1996. After the course and time at the Mayer-Lissmann Opera School, Louise went back to being a Chartered Accountant in corporate life, but still continued singing. She is in demand as a Verdi singer and likes confusing musical directors with her ability to keep swapping between soprano and mezzo roles.

Performance Accountancy is a combination of both professional worlds. The business offers accounting and taxation services to musicians, actors, singers, dancers, voiceover artists as well as other performers, people in the arts, media and entertainment arena, and the creative industry that surrounds them all. As Louise still performs, she has in-depth knowledge of the frustrations of trying to be creative and perform, alongside the administration nightmare that people face in dealing with finance and tax.

In 2017, Performance Accountancy was a finalist in the Accounting Practice Excellence Awards as one of the top five specialist teams for her work with performers, so you know you are in good hands here.

The image of a boring accountant is far from what Performance Accountancy represents.

ACKNOWLEDGEMENTS

I could write a great long Oscar (or Tony) award speech here, which would be quite funny, but I just don't have the skills for that. So here goes:

- ♫ Cybil Collins for my passion for music;

- ♫ My parents for telling me to get a proper career (is being an accountant a proper career?);

- ♫ Karen Williams and the team for nagging me to hit deadlines;

- ♫ Chris Waters for not nagging me to hit deadlines;

- ♫ Dawn and Paul Edwards for plugging some knowledge gaps;

- ♫ The people who reviewed my book before it went to print;

- ♫ For HMRC having a system in that I could take screenshots and put into my book and training course (see licence here: http://www.nationalarchives.gov.uk/doc/open-government-licence/version/3/);

- ♫ Fob Creative for some of the graphics as I am useless at this visual stuff;

- ♫ Verdi for writing Nabucco as that has been my earworm for the last few edits of the book;

♫ And last but not least, you guys for picking up the book in the first place and allowing me to guide you through the pain of being a self-employed performer dealing with accounts and tax, maybe for the first time. Please note – I don't assume you purchased it now!

IT IS NOW
THE END